The Stranger in S

Thomas J. Howell

Alpha Editions

This edition published in 2024

ISBN : 9789362998262

Design and Setting By
Alpha Editions
www.alphaedis.com
Email - info@alphaedis.com

As per information held with us this book is in Public Domain.
This book is a reproduction of an important historical work. Alpha Editions uses the best technology to reproduce historical work in the same manner it was first published to preserve its original nature. Any marks or number seen are left intentionally to preserve its true form.

HISTORY.

THE carelessness which in many instances is evident in the orthography of our ancestors, frequently renders it matter of extreme difficulty to fix, with accuracy and precision, the etymology of places which in early times were conspicuous for the parts they bore in our national transactions.

This is in some measure the situation of Shrewsbury, which by the ancient Welsh was called Ymwithig, or "the Delight;" by the Britons Pengwern; and by the Saxons Scrobbesbyrig; the two latter names signifying nearly the same, "the Head of the Alder Groves." But it is probable that the Normans after their conquest of the Island, either from inability to pronounce the harsher Saxon words, or from the spirit of innovation on the names and manners of the inhabitants, generally possessed by conquerors, were induced to soften the term into Shrobbesburie and Sloppesburie, from whence were derived the modern names of Shrewsbury and Salop, in latin Salopia. Some are inclined to think the latter name was formed from the two Saxon words *sel*, signifying pleasant, and *hope*, the side of a hill, which certainly accords with its situation.

Leland, the antiquary and poet, in his description of the town, thus accounts for its name:—

> Built on a hill, fair Salop greets the eye,
> While Severn forms a crescent gliding by;
> Two bridges cross the navigable stream,
> And British Alders gave the town a name.

Although much doubt remains relative to the founder of Shrewsbury, it is certain that "it was repaired about the year 552 by Maelgwyn, king of North Wales;" and the most probable conjecture is, that it was erected between the years 520 and 594 by the Britons, in order to protect themselves from the bloody ravages and harrassing incursions of the Saxons who had previously levelled the Roman Uriconium (the present Wroxeter) and its fortress with the ground, and forced them to retreat beyond the Severn, which then became the boundary of the kingdom of Mercia.

The Britons having established themselves on the hill Pengwerne, founded a city, which became the metropolis of that part of Wales called Powis, one of the princes of which, Brochwell Ysithroc, had his residence here in 617, and thence it was named Pengwerne Powis.—The blood-thirsty spirit of their Saxon invaders still pursued them: after several dreadful and sanguinary contests with the merciless Offa, the British Prince was at length compelled to abandon the patrimony of his ancestors and retire to Mathrafal, amidst the mountains of Montgomeryshire, after witnessing the destruction of his princely mansion, which stood on the spot lately occupied by the church of St. Chad; and finally, in 777, to surrender that part of the country situated between the Severn and a deep dyke and high rampart, extending 0 miles over roads and mountains and across deep vallies and rivers, which Offa threw up as a new boundary between them and Mercia.

In the reign of Alfred, Shrewsbury was numbered among the British cities, by the name of Caer Pengwerne; and during that of Edward the elder, a mint was established here, as appears from a piece of coin now in preservation, with this inscription, *Edward Rex Angliæ*, and on the reverse *Aelmaer on Scrobe*.

Ethelred, with his court, kept the Christmas of 1006 at Shrewsbury, and being unable to resist the perpetual attacks of the Danes, then invading England under Swaine, he summoned a council here, by whose advice he paid £30,000, to procure a temporary and inglorious peace. About the same time Alfhelm, a prince of the blood, was invited to a banquet here by Edric, duke of Mercia and whilst hunting in the neighbourhood was murdered by one Godwin Porthund, a butcher, at the instigation of Edric, and from whence it is supposed arose the custom, recited in Doomsday Book, that whenever the king was here, twelve of the chief citizens should guard his person during his residence in the city, and attend him when he enjoyed himself with the pleasures of the chase.

In the year 1016, the inhabitants having revolted to Canute, Edmund, afterwards, when king surnamed Ironside, marched quickly hither from the north, and having taken the city, exercised every species of cruelty on them as a punishment for their revolt.

No material transactions appear to have occurred in the annals of Shrewsbury for nearly half a century, from the last named date until the conquest of England by the Normans under William. The city was then granted, together with nearly the whole of the county and a great proportion of land in other parts of the kingdom, to Roger de Montgomery, a Norman chief related to William, and by whom he was attended in his English expedition. Roger was no sooner put in possession of his newly acquired property, than being sensible of the advantages resulting from the situation of the town, he constituted it the capital of his earldom, and fixed his abode in it as lord paramount of the county; and having judiciously built a castle on the isthmus, for the purpose of protecting his residence from the attack of his enemies, with the assistance of inferior barons of his court, administered various solemn and kingly acts of justice, donation, and investiture within its walls. Earl Roger was, however, not suffered to enjoy the immense possessions bestowed on him by the Norman conqueror without molestation: Owen Gwynedd, a spirited Welsh chieftain, excited either by hopes of plunder or a desire to dispossess the invaders, of a place which was capable of being rendered a great annoyance to his countrymen in the hands of powerful enemies, attacked it with a considerable body of Welsh; and so important was his attack considered by William, that he marched with a numerous army from the north, for the purpose of repelling the daring disturber; nor did his usual good fortune desert him in this instance, Owen being defeated and a great portion of his followers slain. As a suitable acknowledgment to divine providence for his good fortune and the splendid triumphs of his arms, the Earl founded the benedictine Abbey of St. Peter and St. Paul. A short time previous to his death he was shorn a monk. He died July 27th, 1094, and was buried in the chapel of the Abbey; over his tomb was placed an armed knight in stone.

Robert de Belesme, son of Roger de Montgomery, who succeeded his brother Hugh the Red in the earldom of Shrewsbury, united with the party who wished to seat Robert, duke of Normandy, on the throne, in lieu of Henry the First; and on the coronation of that monarch, openly rebelled against his authority, placing the castle under the command of Roger de Corbet, and garrisoning it with 80 soldiers. Henry immediately marched for Shrewsbury at the head of 60,000 men, and threatening, if the town was not delivered up to him in three days, to hang all he should find therein, Robert surrendered, and sent the keys to the king by Ralph, abbot of Seez, imploring his clemency: this was granted, but Robert was banished to Normandy, his immense estates forfeited, and the splendour of his baronial house for ever extinguished. Henry then took the government of the town into his own hands, and granted the inhabitants their first charter.—The restless disposition of Robert however still incited him to fresh acts of rebellion, but being taken prisoner, he was brought over to England, and being sentenced to perpetual imprisonment, he at length died a miserable death in Wareham castle.

In 1116, the nobility of the realm did homage to William, Henry's son, at Shrewsbury, and swore allegiance to his father.

The conquest of Wales had always been a leading object in the politics of England, not only from the desire of more extensive dominion, but as a means of preventing in future the devastation and misery which the animosity of a warlike and injured people had occasioned on the English borders. The utility likewise of employing in foreign enterprises a martial nobility, inclined the Norman princes to encourage, by every incitement of advantage and honour, the dangerous designs of subduing or of making settlements in Wales. The consequence of the attacks of the rapacious Norman barons on the Welsh was, that Shrewsbury was continually subject to the ravages and injuries of the contending parties. Besides this, its natural strength and situation on the borders, or as they were then termed the Marches of Wales, rendered it extremely eligible for the rendezvous of the army employed in the Principality, and it was therefore frequently honoured with the presence of those who swayed the sceptre of Britain.

During the struggles between Stephen and the empress Maud, William Fitz Alan, governor of the castle of Shrewsbury, espoused the cause of the latter, and being joined by several noblemen and gentlemen in these parts, left his castle in the care of a deputy, from whom he exacted an oath that he would not deliver up his charge to the king. Stephen having taken the castle, and hanged several of the garrison for the obstinacy of their defence, Alan was forced to fly, leaving his castle and estates in the possession of the king; but on the accession of Henry II. he was restored to all his honours and estates, for his faithful adherence to the fortunes of the family.

In the beginning of the reign of king John, a royal council was assembled in Shrewsbury for the purpose of devising means to put a stop to the continual and harrassing incursions of the Welsh. Gwenwynwyn, prince of Powis, offered terms of reconciliation, but, without any apparent cause, he was detained a prisoner.—The Welsh shortly after attempted to recover their liberties; on this occasion John assembled a large army at Oswestry, and released Gwenwynwyn and several other Welsh chieftains, who immediately repaired to his standard with all the forces they could muster. Llewellin ap Jorwerth, who then governed Wales, was obliged to retire before this powerful army of the British monarch, and delivered hostages to answer for the rectitude of his conduct. But Llewellin, fired with the idea of rescuing his countrymen from the yoke of foreign government, once more broke the truce which had been concluded.

When intelligence of this event reached John, his heart was so steeled against the feelings of humanity that he ordered the immediate execution of the hostages, 28 in number, and chiefly children allied to the first families in Wales—a deed which renders his name worthy to be recorded on the same page, in the annals of cruelty, with that of Nero. Nottingham was the place in which this tragical drama was acted, and from thence John marched with his army for the purpose of chastising the Welsh; but fear and distrust took possession of his mind, and learning that the Pope had dissolved the allegiance of his subjects, he dismissed his army on a sudden and returned to London. Llewellin soon after suddenly appeared before Shrewsbury, which he now entered without opposition; nor did a long period elapse before the Welsh took ample vengeance for the cruelties committed on their countrymen. An insurrection having broke out in England, in consequence of the unpopular ministry of Peter de Roche bishop of Winchester, in the 17th of Henry III. many of the barons joined Llewellin, and having united their forces, laid waste the Marches, and entering Shrewsbury, after having plundered and burnt the town, in which were considerable riches, they put many of the inhabitants to the sword. Notwithstanding peace was established between the contending monarchs, the national jealousies and deep rooted hatred of the two nations were the fruitful source of perpetual conflicts, to repress which, Henry marched with his array to Shrewsbury, where, in 1269, peace was again restored, through the mediation of the Pope's legate; and the town and castle of Shrewsbury were placed under the care of Edward, the king's eldest son, afterwards the celebrated Edward I.

On the death of his father, Edward succeeded to the throne, and determined to exert every effort which his power and talents afforded, to obtain what had long been the object of his ambition, the entire conquest of Wales. Soon after Easter, 1277, Edward left London to regulate the measures of the ensuing campaign; and that the administration of justice might not be delayed, by the absence of the king and the length of the war, he removed the Court of Exchequer and the Court of King's Bench to Shrewsbury.

In the general accommodation made with the vanquished followers of Simon de Montfort, earl of Leicester, in 1264, Llewellin ap Gryffydd was included; but he saw that a blow was meditating by the English king, which though suspended for a time, would be the more severe, and fall with greater weight on his country. Llewellin thought it prudent to secure the support of the adherents of the house of Montfort, of whom many yet remained in England by solemnizing his marriage with the daughter of the late earl. He therefore demanded the young lady from the French king, to whose court on the demise of her father she had retired, but on her passage to Wales she was taken by some of the English vessels and detained at the court of Edward. Llewellin demanded the fulfilment of a treaty made between Henry III. and himself and the release of his bride from Edward, while the latter required Llewellin to appear and do homage for his kingdom, which he refused to perform unless hostages were delivered for the safety of his person. This was the ostensible cause of the war undertaken by Edward, and the pretext for attempting an entire conquest of the principality. Edward cautiously avoided putting to the test the well known valour of a nation inflamed with a just sense of their wrongs and proud of their ancient independence.—Llewellin unable to face an enemy pressing on by slow, cautious, and decisive operations, returned to the mountains of Snowdon, and Edward not choosing to enter the recesses of that difficult country, calmly awaited the result of his policy. The prospect of a famine seconded his prudential schemes, and Llewellin had no better alternative than to implore the clemency of the English monarch. Little generosity or pity was to be expected in the terms granted by Edward, and accordingly Llewellin agreed to pay 5000 marks as a fine; to do homage for his crown; to relinquish all the country between Chester and the river Conway; and to deliver hostages for his future submission.

On his return to London, Edward was attended by the Welsh prince and a numerous retinue of chieftains, for the purpose of swearing fealty to their conqueror. During their stay they were continual subjects of derision to the populace, who treated them as savages and laughed at their foreign garb and unusual appearance. To a people proud and irascible, and who, though vanquished, were still alive to injury and insult—to a sense of their own valour, and to the fond idea of their native independence, this treatment could not be pleasing. They therefore, privately entered into an agreement to revolt on the first opportunity; resolving to die in their own country as freemen, rather than come any more as vassals into England, to be the sport of a haughty and contemptuous nation. Accordingly they flew to arms. Edward, surprised to find himself again attacked by the Welsh prince, determined to crush effectually the rebellious spirit of the Welsh, and advanced from Shrewsbury with a considerable army. The progress of the king was at first slow, in consequence of several advantages gained over him by Llewellin, but the latter being at length surprised near Builth, in Brecknockshire, he was defeated, and together with 2000 of his soldiers, slain. Gratitude could pay no tribute to his memory so expressive, as the tears which his country shed upon the tomb of their prince, who, after many efforts to preserve the freedom of the land which gave him birth, fell in the conflict, and found an honorable grave in its ruins.

David who had previously forgotten the feuds which disturbed the peace of his family and country, assumed, on the death of his brother, the sovereignty of North Wales; but after various unsuccessful struggles, he was basely betrayed into the hands of Edward, who confined him in Rhuddlan castle, and soon after sent him in chains to Shrewsbury.

Edward now (1283) summoned a parliament to meet at Shrewsbury, for "consulting what course to take with David prince of Wales," whence, in a few days it was removed to Acton Burnell. David, whilst at the English Court had been made a baron of the realm, and it was in consequence determined to proceed against him as a subject of the crown. His judges, deaf to the claims of humanity and justice, and influenced, no doubt, by their desire to gratify the implacable and vindictive spirit of their master, condemned him to die as a traitor. For this act of revenge, new tortures were invented.—He was sentenced to be drawn at a horse's tail through the town—to be hanged—his heart and bowels to be burnt—his head to be cut off, and exposed at the tower of London, and his body quartered and hung up in different parts of the kingdom. On the death of this prince, the Welsh every where submitted to the victorious arms of the conqueror.

The tragical and cruel death of David closed the only sovereignty which remained of the ancient British empire: an empire which through various changes of fortune, had opposed the disciplined legions of imperial Rome; and for more than eight hundred years, had valiantly withstood the most strenuous efforts of their Saxon and Norman invaders.

The conquest of Wales by the English monarch was of great importance to Shrewsbury, the inhabitants of which had now time for breathing, after having been for nearly 800 years in the scene of continual warfare.

Edward II. visited Shrewsbury in 1322, on his march to subdue the barons who had justly banished the Spencers and was met by the burgesses in armour, who escorted him into the town. About this period, John, one of the sons of the famous Roger Mortimer, earl of March, was slain in a tournament held here. In 1326, Edmund Fitz Alan, earl of Arundel, who had been a faithful adherent of the weak and unfortunate Edward, was apprehended in the neighbourhood of this place by the partizans of the abandoned Queen and her paramour Roger Mortimer.

Richard II. who appears to have been particularly attached to the inhabitants of these marches, summoned a parliament to assemble at Shrewsbury in 1397, and which is called by Speed the "great parliament," in consequence of the extraordinary number of peers who assembled here. The king was sumptuously entertained, and the parliament too much devoted to his interests, passed several very oppressive acts. One of the articles of accusation on which he was afterwards deposed, charges him with "procuring the many oppressive acts passed in the parliament of Shrewsbury, and with intimidating the judges and other persons whom he caused to come before him there."

In the following reign the Welsh made another attempt to recover their freedom under the celebrated Owen Glyndwr. Twice were Henry and his generals obliged to retire from their meditated attack of Owen without bringing him to any action, and his rebellion assumed a more serious appearance from the support which he received from the earls of Northumberland and Worcester, and the earl of Douglas, who were disgusted with the treatment which they had received from Henry. At the commencement of the war, Northumberland was suddenly taken ill at Berwick—Hotspur his son accordingly took the command of the troops, amounting to about 12,000 chosen men, and marched towards Shrewsbury to unite his forces with those of the Welsh chieftain. The king aware of the importance of every moment, also hurried to Shrewsbury, and interposed himself between Hotspur and Glyndwr. This moment saved his crown;

and the prudence of the one leader and the impetuosity of the other induced them to hasten a general engagement.

Previous to the engagement, Henry sent Thomas Presbury, abbot of Shrewsbury, with offers of pardon to Percy's army if they would disperse, but this message being misrepresented to Percy by the earl of Worcester, the former sent a manifesto into the royal army in which he renounced his allegiance to Henry and enumerated at length various grievances and indignities of which he conceived the nation in common with his own family had to complain. This manifesto tended to inflame the passions of both parties; and the ability of the respective commanders, the valour of the soldiers and their equality in point of numbers, gave reason to expect a dreadful and doubtful contest. The battle was fought at Oldfield or Bullfield, now Battlefield, about 3 miles north of Shrewsbury, on St. Magdalene's eve, July 22, 1403. The onset commenced near Berwick with a terrible discharge of arrows from both lines. The Scots rushed with impetuous fury upon the front of the royal army, which began to give way, but the king arriving with reinforcements they again rallied and recovered their ground. Henry exposed his person in the thickest of the fight and combated with an ardour worthy the crown he was defending. His valiant son whose military achievements in France were afterwards so renowned and whose wild youthful excesses are so beautifully pourtrayed by our great dramatic bard, here performed his noviciate in arms, signalized himself on his father's footsteps, and regained his good opinion. The gallant Percy supported that brilliant fame he had acquired in so many bloody engagements, and Douglas,

> Whose high deeds,
> Whose hot incursions, and great name in arms
> Holds from all soldiers chief majority,

the ancient enemy of Percy but now his friend, still appeared his rival amidst the horror and confusion of the day. This nobleman performed feats of valour which are almost incredible. He seemed determined that the king of England should that day fall by his arm: and as Henry either to elude the attacks of the enemy on his person, or to encourage his own men by the belief of his presence every where, had accoutred several captains in the royal garb; the sword of Douglas rendered this proud distinction fatal to many. Having dispatched sir Walter Blount, the king's standard bearer, he assailed Henry with such fury that it was with difficulty he escaped to another part of the field. But while the armies were contending in this furious manner, the death of Percy by an unknown hand, decided the fate of the day and the royalists prevailed. On this memorable day, which is immortalized by the genius of Shakspeare, it is supposed that 7000 men were slain. A great number of persons of distinction were killed on both aides, and the earls of Douglas and Worcester, taken prisoners; the latter was after beheaded at Shrewsbury.

This battle, which fixed the house of Lancaster on the throne during three reigns, is among those of the first importance recorded in ancient English history, and may be named as the first of those conflicts between the white and red roses, which some years after deluged the nation with some of its best blood, and filled it with intestine ravages and divisions.

Owen Glyndwr had the mortification to be obliged to remain inactive at the head of his troops at Oswestry, from whence he retired on hearing of Percy's defeat: and although he afterwards attempted, he was unable to regain the independence of his native country.—He died in Herefordshire in 1414. Henry returned thanks to heaven for this brilliant victory, and founded the collegiate church at Battlefield on the spot where it is probable most of the slain were buried.

During the fatal quarrel between the houses of York and Lancaster, which is computed to have cost the lives of eighty princes of the blood, and to have almost entirely annihilated the ancient nobility of England, Shrewsbury remained steadily attached to the Yorkists, and previous to the battle of St. Albans, Richard Plantagenet, duke of York wrote to his "right worshipful friends the bailiffs, burgesses and commoners of the good town of Shrewsbury," requesting assistance in his enterprise for the recovery of his throne. After his defeat and death at Wakefield, his son Edward, earl of March, appeared in Shrewsbury, entreating a supply of men to revenge his father's death. With an army of 23,000 men chiefly raised in this neighbourhood, he obtained a decisive victory at Mortimer's Cross in Herefordshire, from whence advancing rapidly to London he was shortly afterwards proclaimed king. Edward, duly sensible of the strength and inviolable attachment of Shrewsbury to his cause, committed the care of his queen to its inhabitants, and during her residence here she twice lay in at the convent of the Black Friars, and was delivered of Richard and George Plantagenet, the former of whom was murdered in the Tower through the cruelty of his uncle Richard III. and the latter died young.

In 1484, Henry Stafford, duke of Buckingham, having entered into a conspiracy for the purpose of depriving Richard of a throne which he had acquired by such manifold injustice, and his endeavours being frustrated, fled to the house of one Bannister, at Shinewood, near Wenlock, in order to concealment, but notwithstanding Bannister was indebted to the duke for the property he enjoyed, unable to withstand the temptation of so large a reward as £1000, basely betrayed him to John Mitton, esq. then sheriff of the county, who conducted him to Shrewsbury, where Richard shortly after arrived, and feasted his eyes with the execution of his enemy.

The crimes of Richard were so horrid and so shocking to humanity that the natural sentiments of men, without any political or public views, were sufficient to render his government unstable; and every person of probity and honour, earnest to prevent the sceptre from being any longer polluted by the bloody and faithless hand which held it, at length united in favour of the earl of Richmond. This nobleman set sail from Harfleur, in France, on the 7th of August, 1484, and landed at Milford Haven, in Pembrokeshire, without opposition, with about 2000 followers. He directed his course to that part of the kingdom in hopes that the Welsh, who regarded him as their countryman, and who had been already prepossessed in favour of his cause by means of the late duke of Buckingham, would join his standard. Richard, not knowing where to expect his antagonist, took post at Nottingham, and purposed to fly on the first alarm to the place exposed to danger. He had appointed sir Rice ap Thomas and sir Walter Herbert to defend the coasts of Wales; but the former joined Richmond, and the latter made scarcely any resistance. The earl advanced towards Shrewsbury, which was the only convenient place at which he could cross the Severn, but very unexpectedly found the gates shut against him; and on his demanding entrance by his herald, he was refused, "the head bailey, Maister Myttoon, being a stoute wyse gentilman," saying, "that he knew no kynge, but only kynge Richard, whose lyffetenants he and hys fellows were; and before he should entir there, he should go over hys belly, meaninge thereby, that he would be slayne to the ground, and that he protested vehementlye on the othe he had tacken; but on better advice, Maister Myttoon permitted the kynge to pass; but to save his othe, the sayd Myttoon lay alonge the grounde, and his belly upwardes, and soe the sayd erle stepped over hym and saved hys othe." Previous to his reaching Shrewsbury his army scarcely deserved that name, from their wretched appearance and small numbers; but being joined by sir Gilbert Talbot with 2000 of the tenants of his nephew, the earl of Shrewsbury, together with several gentlemen of rank, his cause began to wear a favourable aspect, and marching on with his army, now amounting to about 6000 men Richmond gained the brilliant and decisive victory of Bosworth; Richard perishing by a fate too mild and honourable for his multiplied and detestable enormities.

It is supposed by some that that plague, the sweating sickness, which broke out here in 1485, originated among Henry's foreign levies; it afterwards infested the kingdom at different periods for 60 years: and, according to Mr. Pennant, Shrewsbury particularly felt its ravages, 1000 nearly dying per day at one period.

Henry was not unmindful of the reception he met with here, and, when quietly seated on the throne, several times visited the town, particularly in

1495, when he was sumptuously entertained in the castle by the corporation.

Nothing worthy of note in the history occurs from this period until the struggle between the Parliament and Charles I.; the former for their privileges and the rights of the people, and the latter for arbitrary power as a despotic monarch. Charles, determined to try the force of arms, erected the royal standard at Nottingham, the open signal of discord and civil war throughout the kingdom. Whilst many of the large towns and corporate bodies took part with the parliament, a great proportion of the nobility and gentry sided with the king; the latter was the case with the Salopians. Not meeting with the support which he expected in the vicinity of Nottingham, Charles after a little hesitation pursued his march to Shrewsbury "in regard of the strong and pleasant situation of it, one side being defended by the Severn, the other having secure passage into Wales;" having received information that the place was entirely devoted to him.

At Wellington the king passed one night, and on the following morning made a rendezvous of all his forces on the plain beneath the Wrekin. His orders having been read at the head of each regiment, he placed himself in the midst of his army, and that he might bind himself by reciprocal ties, he solemnly made the following declaration in their presence; "I do promise, in the presence of Almighty God, and as I hope for his blessing and protection, that I will, to the utmost of my power, defend and maintain the true reformed protestant religion, established in the church of England, and by the grace of God, in the same will live and die. I desire that the laws may ever be the measure of my government, and that the liberty and property of the subject may be preserved by them with the same care as my own just rights. And if it please God by his blessing on this army raised for my necessary defence to preserve me from the present rebellion, I do solemnly and faithfully promise in the sight of God, to maintain the just privileges and freedom of parliament, and to govern to the utmost of my power, by the known statutes and customs of the kingdom, and particularly to observe inviolably the laws to which I have given my consent this parliament. Mean while, if this emergency and the great necessity to which I am driven, beget any violation of law, I hope it shall be imputed by God and man to the authors of this war; not to me, who have so earnestly laboured to preserve the peace of the kingdom. When I willingly fail in these particulars, I shall expect no aid or relief from man, nor any protection from above; but in this resolution I hope for the cheerful assistance of all good men, and am confident of the blessing of Heaven." Had Charles previously acted up to this declaration, he would not now have been placed in such a critical situation.

Although the tyrannical proceedings of the king had induced many of the Salopians to look upon his cause in an unfavourable light, yet his mild and amiable behaviour won on the inhabitants generally, so much so that a considerable number enrolled themselves as volunteers in his service. In order to give efficiency to his troops and maintain his cause, a mint was established here for the purpose of coining the plate which had been presented to him by various public bodies and private individuals; but at such a low ebb were the mechanic arts at this period, that scarcely £1000 per week could be coined.

However despicable the royal army appeared when it marched from Nottingham, its improvement was rapid on its arrival in Shrewsbury, so that in about twenty days it mustered 12000 men, chiefly persons of considerable property, from the neighbouring parts. But they were exceedingly ill equipped, for says Clarendon; "In the whole body not a pikeman had a corselet, and very few musketeers had swords."—Add to this, that there was not a single tent, and very few waggons attached to the whole train. With this ill accoutred but high spirited body, Charles took his leave of Shrewsbury, on the 12th of October, 1642.

On the departure of the king, a garrison was left in town, of which Lord Capel was appointed governor, and a fort was erected on an eminence above Frankwell, to secure that quarter from attack. Capel was severally succeeded by Sir Fulke Hunkes (a relative of the celebrated Baxter, the non-conformist,) Sir Richard Otteley, and Sir Michael Earnley. This gentleman was in a very declining state of health, in consequence of which many disorders crept in among the garrison, and gave the commanders of the parliamentary forces in the neighbourhood, opportunity to attempt the conquest of so important a post. After two unsuccessful attempts by Colonels Mitton, and Langhorne, two enterprising officers, they at length attained the object of their wishes. Having arrived before the town with fifteen hundred picked men of the garrisons of Wem and Oswestry, they contrived to convey eight carpenters up the river, who were landed within a breast work on the east side of the castle hill, and notwithstanding they were fired on by the centinels, they continued to cut down a sufficient quantity of palisadoes to enable the troops to enter. After storming a rampart beneath the Council House, a large body of troops entered by St. Mary's Water-Lane, where the guard, having been intoxicated or bribed, made no resistance. Having opened the north gate, the horse immediately marched in, commanded by Cols. Mitton and Bowyer.—The consternation of the inhabitants may be easily imagined. The preceding night they had retired to rest, confident in their supposed security, but by daylight in the morning they were in the hands of their enemies; and, notwithstanding the humane exertions of Col. Mitton, the soldiery were not to be restrained from plundering the peaceably disposed of their private property. The first intimation which the governor received of the surprise of the town, was the entrance of some of his enemies into his chamber, where he fell covered with wounds, repeatedly refusing quarter, being determined not to outlive the disgrace of the day. The English part of the garrison were suffered to march to Ludlow, but the Irish were left to the discretion of Col. Mitton. The fort at Frankwell bravely held out till night, but finding resistance useless, at length surrendered at discretion. A number of prisoners of rank were taken, besides 15 pieces of cannon, a large stand of arms, and the whole of prince Maurice's magazine. Nor did the plate and valuable effects of many of the surrounding gentry, placed in the castle for security, during the turbulence of the times, meet a better fate: the whole of it to a vast amount, falling into the hands of the victors. For this important achievement, Colonel Mitton received the thanks of Parliament. The fall of Shrewsbury was a death blow to Charles's expectations in this quarter; for besides its being the key to North Wales, it caused the dissolution of a formidable confederacy between the counties of Salop, Worcester, Chester and Flint, then on the eve of assembling to defend the falling fortunes of their king.

After the battle of Worcester, so fatal to the royal cause, a commission was sent to Chester by the Parliament, to try the Earl of Derby, and other gentlemen on charges of treason and rebellion; or in other words, for having borne arms in defence of Charles. One of these was Colonel John Benbow, who, in the beginning of the contest, had united with the parliamentary army, and distinguished himself at the surprise of Shrewsbury. Afterwards, disgusted with the violent proceedings against the king, and perceiving that the object of the leaders of his party was private aggrandizement, and not the welfare of their country, he left them and repaired to the royal standard. This was a crime which could not be pardoned; he was therefore condemned to death. That his punishment might be rendered most bitter, the sentence was pronounced by Colonel Mackworth, once his friend and fellow soldier; and it was ordered to be executed at his native town of Shrewsbury, that a terrible impression might be made on the inhabitants of that loyal place. He was shot on the green before the castle, October 15, 1651, and suffered with great intrepidity. This respectable officer was uncle to the celebrated admiral Benbow.

An unsuccessful attempt was made to surprise the castle, in order to favour the restoration of Charles the second, in 1654, but it ended merely in plunging the king's friends still deeper in misery and ruin: among the most active in this enterprise was Sir Thomas Harris, who suffered most severely for his well intended zeal. After Cromwell's death, and the restoration of the long parliament, upon Sir George Booth's rising in Cheshire for the king, the venerable Sir Thomas Middleton, then 80 years of age, proclaimed him at Wrexham, which so much encouraged the royalists of Shropshire and Denbighshire, that they immediately sent a party to seize Shrewsbury, but though the friends of monarchy were very numerous in it, Captain Edmund Waringe of Oldbury, the governor, prevented their design, and secured the place for the parliament. In 1683, when the nation was thrown into a ferment, by the discovery of the Rye House Plot, this town was one of those which the conspirators, presuming on its general disaffection to the government of Charles the second, proposed to have seized. Such at least was the deposition of the infamous Colonel Romsey, a wretch on whose head lies the blood of the virtuous and patriotic Russel—who adds, in his narrative, that there were in the castle 38 barrels of powder, 138 pounds in the barrel, with arms for 300 men and great guns. "The castle," he, observes, "is strong by situation, and lies so conveniently, that either from the north or west, or Midland, or Wales, the rebellious party might easily resort thither."

The last royal visit paid to this town was by the bigotted James the second, who passed the 25th of August, 1687, here, and kept his court at the Council House. The sentiments of loyal attachment, for which Shrewsbury has ever been conspicuous, burst forth on this occasion, with chivalrous enthusiasm.—They blazed in bonfires and illuminations, and literally ran through the streets in torrents of wine, the public conduits being charged with this royal liquid.

Having brought down the general history of Shrewsbury to a late date, we shall now proceed to view its local character. There is no doubt that its Trade was formerly very considerable, and though its importance in this respect may have been eclipsed by the more eligible situation of numerous other places for the manufacture of various articles, it has never ceased to enjoy a considerable share of internal commerce. Heylyn speaks of it as "a fair and goodly town, well traded and frequented by all sorts of people, both Welsh and English, by reason of the *trade of cloth*, and other Merchandise; it being the common mart or emptory between Wales and England," and Mr. Pennant, who wrote his account of Shrewsbury above 40 years ago, gives the following account of its trade in Welsh woollens: "From very early days this place possessed almost exclusively the trade with Wales in a coarse kind of woollen cloth called Welsh webs, which were brought from Merioneth and Montgomeryshires to a market held here weekly on Thursday. They were afterwards dressed, that is, the wool raised on one side, by a set of people called Shearmen. At the time of Queen Elizabeth, the trade was so great, that not fewer than 600 persons maintained themselves by this occupation. The cloth was sent chiefly to America to clothe the negroes, or to Flanders; where it is used by the peasants. At present the greatest part of this traffic is diverted into other channels, and not more than 4 or 5000 yards are brought to the ancient mart." This market is now entirely done away, through an unfortunate disagreement between the manufacturers of these articles and the drapers of Shrewsbury, and the market is now held at Welsh Pool every other Thursday. The mode of raising the wool on one side, described by Mr. Pennant, being found to be injurious to the texture of the cloth, the number of shearman has considerable declined, insomuch that there are only a few in the town at this time. Beside, its trade in Welsh flannels and webs, a brewery appears to have been established here in 1618; and in the reign of Henry VIII. and Elizabeth it was famous for its glove and shoe manufactory.

Nor is the trade carried on in Shrewsbury at this period inconsiderable—being the capital of a large and populous county, its vicinity to the principality of Wales, and the facility with which articles of every description are forwarded either by land or water carriage, render it an extensive mart for the disposal of goods. Here are two very large linen factories, besides manufactories for starch, soap, flannels, cotton goods, an extensive iron and brass foundry, two ale and porter breweries, a spirit distillery, &c. which will be noticed under their proper heads, as well as various mechanical trades which are common to all other large towns, and which contribute in no small degree to the accumulation of wealth, to the enjoyment of the conveniences of life, and to the power of benevolent actions by the inhabitants.

Shrewsbury is also famed for its excellent brawn and a kind of sweet flat cake, whose good qualities are celebrated by the elegant pen of Shenstone,

> "For here each season do those cakes abide,
> Whose honoured names the inventive city own,
> Rend'ring thro' Britain's isle, Salopia's praises known."

With the increase of trade and riches we must also connect that of its population and its consequent extension of buildings. In the reign of Edward the Confessor there were only 252 houses here, and the earliest calculation of the number of inhabitants on record is in 1695; the town then contained 7383 persons—in 1750, there were 8141 inhabitants and 1884 houses. In the years 1801, 1811, and 1821, enumerations were made, agreeable to orders of the House of Commons, and which are here subjoined:

1801.		1811.		1821.	
Inhabit.	*Houses.*	*Inhabit.*	*Houses.*	*Inhabit.*	*Houses.*

| 13,479. | 2,861. | 15,542. | 3,024. | 18,242. | 3,463. |

From these statements it appears that an increase of 2063 persons took place in the first 10 years, and 2700 in the second, but it should be observed that as each parish extends more or less into the surrounding country, it is probable that the town does not contain more than 16,000 inhabitants.

Although much remains to be done in order to put Shrewsbury on an equality, with respect to elegance and convenience, with many other places not its superiors in size, wealth, or situation, numerous praise-worthy improvements have taken place during the last 60 years. Previous to that period there was but one Inn (the Raven) of any extent for the accommodation of strangers, no stage coach; neither cart nor waggon was employed for the conveyance of goods, packhorses being only in use; and such persons as had occasion to travel were obliged to perform their journies on horseback, postchaises being unknown.—At length about 1761 the first stage coach made its appearance in Shrewsbury, and since that period by the indefatigable perseverance of the late Mr. Robert Lawrence, of the Lion Inn, in completing the communications and bettering the roads: a noble and substantial Guildhall, two beautiful stone bridges over the river Severn, together with two new and elegant churches, and a great number of charitable and benevolent erections have given additional beauty to this interesting and venerable town. Its suburbs have been materially enlarged and improved, many obstructions in the principal streets removed, and the facilities for travelling have been astonishingly increased.

The government and police of Shrewsbury have the next claim on our attention. It is a corporation by prescription, and charters have been granted to it by almost every king of England since William the Norman. The first regular charter was granted by Henry I.; this was confirmed by John, who in addition empowered the burgesses to chuse two prœpositi of bailiffs removeable only on bad behaviour; but it was not until Edward III. that the bailiffs were constituted magistrates and authorised to hold a session for the trial of causes. The institution of aldermen is supposed have taken place in the 12th of Richard II. for "about the year 1390, the earl of Arundel being commissioned by the king to end certain disputes among the Burgesses, awarded that for the good government of the town for the future, the commonalty should elect out of themselves twelve of the most sufficient persons who should continue in their office for two years from the feast of St. Giles."

By the charter of Charles I. granted in 1638, the corporation was new modelled changing the offices of bailiffs into that of a mayor, recorder, steward, town clerk, 24 aldermen, 48 assistants or common councilmen, two chamberlains, a sword bearer, serjeants at mace, &c. &c.; and that the mayor, bishop of Lichfield and Coventry, recorder, steward, 3 senior aldermen, and the alderman who last served the office of mayor, should act as Justices within the town and liberties of Shrewsbury. In this form it now exists. The right of electing the corporate officers is vested in the common council by whom the mayor is chosen annually on the Friday after St. Bartholomew. The general session is held quarterly by the justices of the peace for the borough; and the mayor or some of the aldermen and justices attend the Exchequer every Tuesday to transact public business. A court of requests, for the recovery of debts under the value of forty shillings, is held in the town hall every other Wednesday. The number of its commissioners is about 30, the eligibility for election to which office consists in residence in the town and the possession of freehold property of the value of £30 per annum, or a personal estate of £600 value clear of all deductions.

Notwithstanding the corporation is empowered to enact laws for the most effectual administration of the police of the town, this branch of internal government is in a very disorganized state; yet the many useful regulations which have been established, and the strict and impartial manner in which they are enforced, reflect the greatest credit on the magistrates and conduce to the peaceable demeanour of the inhabitants and the order and respectability of the town. But the most impartial observer will see that much remains to be done for the prevention of immorality; and though it is impossible that the most enlightened, active and persevering magistracy, aided by the continued exertions of the inhabitants can prevent individual delinquency, something may yet be achieved for the preservation of public morals, some plan devised which may foster the sparks of pure and proper feeling as an antidote to that national dereliction of manners in which Shrewsbury in common with most other large towns participates too much.

In addition to the Corporation here are sixteen chartered companies, consisting of various trades, to exercise any of which, within the liberties, no person is admitted who has not either served a legal apprenticeship or paid a sum of money, entitled, "a foreigner's fine", which is of various amount in the several fraternities.—An ancient ceremony, called the Show, used by these, deserves to be recorded, as perhaps, (with the exception of Coventry) it is the only one of the kind now existing in the kingdom. On the second Monday after Trinity Sunday the various companies assemble in front of the castle, with their wardens, flags, devices, &c. &c., each having at their head some person gaudily dressed; some in representation perhaps of the monarchs who granted their respective charters, whilst others display devices and insignia emblematical of the trades which they practise. The procession being arranged, moves over the Welsh bridge to a piece of ground, on the west side the river, and adjoining the town, called

Kingsland, where each company has its arbour, in which is a cold dinner provided for the entertainment of the mayor and corporation, who visit the various arbours with their attendants, decorated in all "the pomp and circumstance" of office. After spending the evening in festivity and mirth, the several companies retire from Kingsland, much invigorated with the essence of barley corn, and return into town over the English bridge.

This ancient pageant is now fast approaching its dissolution. During the few last years, the master tradesmen have entirely ceased to walk in procession to the ancient spot, and the ceremony is now continued only by the apprentices of the chartered companies most numerous in the town. The custom originated in the celebration of the feast of Corpus Christi, one of the most splendid feasts of the Romish Church. After the reformation, the religious part of the ceremony was discontinued, but one day was still set apart for the express purpose of idleness, jollity and merriment.

The first return of Members of Parliament to represent the town of Shrewsbury appears to have been in the 26th of Edward the first. The right of election is vested in the resident burgesses, paying scot and lot, and not receiving alms: the mayor being the returning officer. The burgesses who polled at the contested election, in 1819, were 688 in number.—The freedom of Shrewsbury (with respect to voting) is acquired by serving seven years apprenticeship to a burgess residing within the liberties, or by birth within the liberties on paying the sum of £7 4s. 0d.; every male child of a burgess, who may be born after his father has been sworn in, can claim his burgessship on the payment of £1 6s., whether born in the town or not. Honorary freedoms may be also given by the body corporate. The members who represent the town of Shrewsbury in the British Parliament, are two in number.

Considered as a place of residence, Shrewsbury has the advantage of a salubrious air and mild temperature. At a short distance from the town in a N.E. aspect, a very accurate observer found the mercury in the thermometer down at 8° in January 1814.—By observations on the variations of the thermometer for one year, the same gentleman found that the mean temperature of the same year was 46°, and that the variations, during the course of the year amounted to 77°, varying from 8° to 83°. In South Carolina, the annual variation has extended to 83°. The winter of this year, it may be recollected, was much colder and the summer hotter than is common at Shrewsbury, and yet the highest degree to which the mercury rose was 85°. In the East Indies, the mercury is frequently at 104°. From accurate observation it appeared, that the medium of the daily variations was nearly regular in its increase till June, and from the close of that month till the end of December was again almost uniformly diminishing. The medium of the daily variations was no more than 6°, whereas in some places they reach 30°. From these statements it appears that we are free from those sudden changes of the atmosphere which generally very much affect, and often prove fatal to, the human frame.

That this is a fact may be inferred from the similar temperature of Shrewsbury with that of Sidmouth, in Devonshire, one of the most healthy places perhaps in this kingdom: In the year 1814, the mean temperature was 47°, only one degree above that of Shrewsbury. This observation is also supported by the tables published by Dr. Price, on Reversionary Payments, in which he proves, from the Bills of Mortality that out of 1000 persons born, there were alive

Age	London.	Northampton.	France.	Vaud, Switzerland.	Shrewsbury.
18	334	459	621	618	555
54	125	218	406	367	326
85	7	13	36	17	41

The relative degrees of vitality are thus shewn in a more perspicuous manner than by any other method and from the above table it is evident that the temperature of Shrewsbury is in most instances nearly equal, and in some superior, to the warm climates of France and Switzerland, and extremely favourable to longevity.

The elevation of the town, together with the purity of its atmosphere and the excellence of its water, renders its situation extremely salubrious. Contagious diseases are very rare. The scarlet fever, measles, hooping cough, &c. are usually very mild. The residents in the immediate vicinity of the Severn are most liable to illness, and in these cases the inflammatory symptoms generally run high. Many parts of the town and its environs may justly be recommended as eligible residences for invalids, who visit Shrewsbury from Ireland, Wales, and various parts of the United Kingdom, to avail themselves of the able medical assistance which the town affords.

Shrewsbury is built on two hills, of easy ascent, which for the most part gently slope to the river Severn; by this stream the ground on which the town stands is formed into a peninsula, the castle being judiciously placed on the isthmus, and thus commanding the entrances to the town.

Like most ether places not of Roman origin, its streets are extremely irregular; nor had its buildings, until within these few years, any claim to superiority, the ancient houses being chiefly built with projections into the public streets—an inconvenience very properly remedied by the elegance of modern erections. Its suburbs have of late years very much increased, and, in conjunction with this, many excellent improvements have been made in removing obstructions from the entrances to the town: but, notwithstanding the natural advantages it possesses, the bad state of its pavement and the filthy picture continually presented by its streets, is a source of poignant regret.

The plain of Shropshire, in which the town is situated, is of considerable extent, divided by the Severn into two unequal portions, and though flat, when compared with the surrounding hills, of a very varied surface. Its greatest length from N. to S. is about 30 miles, comprehending the space between Whitchurch and Church Stretton; its breadth from Oswestry to Coalbrookdale, is about 28 miles. Shrewsbury, when viewed from any of its adjacent eminences, presents a beautiful and interesting scene, and the eye of the spectator is led to survey the most extensive amphitheatre of mountains which perhaps the island can boast. The Wrekin is connected by the gentle hills of Acton Burnel and Frodesley, (over which the gigantic summit of Brown Clee is conspicuous,) with the Lawley and Coredock, generally called the Stretton Hills, from whence the Longmynd, Stiperstones, and Long Mountain, from an uninterrupted chain, with the bold and precipitous cliffs of the Kefn y Castyr, Moel y Golfa, and Breyddin, surmounted by an obelisk in honour of the late gallant Lord Rodney; thence the horizon is bounded by the stupendous Berwin range, losing their blue summits in the clouds; while the northern view is terminated by the humbler but beautiful eminences of Grinshill, Pymhill, Hawkstone, Haughmond, &c., round to the Wrekin. The whole of this vast circle incloses a finely wooded and beautifully diversified champaign country, of gentle hill and dale, studded with numerous gentlemen's seats—watered with various streams—eminently fertile in arable, meadow, and pasture; and amply justifying the eulogium of an ancient British poet, who, after gazing, as he tells us, on the plain of Shropshire, from the height of Charlton Hill, calls it the paradise of *Cymru*. [33] The glittering rays of the Sun gilding the lofty spires of the town—the bold and ancient appearance of its ivy-mantled castle—the lovely pleasure and garden grounds which nearly surround it and gently slope from the mouldering ruins of its once warlike walls to the majestic Severn, which, fringed with lofty tufts of trees of various foliages, "proudly rolls its crystal stream along;" altogether form one of the most picturesque and enchanting prospects any where to be met with. Added to this, the well known salubrity of its air, and the many agreeable promenades which on every side of the town present themselves; and the compiler thinks he will not be esteemed too vain in asserting, that his native town is not surpassed, (though, for aught he knows, it may be equalled,) in point of situation, wholesomeness, and picturesque scenery, by any place of equal size in Great Britain.

The general character and manners of the inhabitants of Shrewsbury, as they assume no characteristic sufficient to distinguish them from those of other towns similarly circumstanced and situated, will not long detain the attention of the visitor. He will not often be disgusted with the petty assumptions of office clothed with a "little brief authority," nor will he be displeased in perceiving, in a large majority of the inhabitants, a considerable portion of civility, hospitality, social intercourse, and liberality of opinion; and if great refinement of manners do not characterise them in the aggregate, the stranger will have employed his leisure to little advantage, who does not soon discover in the town a very extensive share of that frankness, benevolence, and warmth which is a prominent feature in the old-British character. Numbers in the different ranks of society are to be met with whose lives are adorned with the honours due to industry, integrity and virtue; and if we add the munificence with which the various public charities are supported by Salopians in general—who

— Learn the luxury of doing good,

in the diffusion of a part of these superfluities with which a benignant Providence has crowned their labours, the writer thinks he is not saying too much when he observes that benevolence is strongly marked in the general portrait. The different churches and chapels are, on the whole, well attended; and in few towns of equal size is there a more decent and orderly observance of the Sabbath. It is, however, to be regretted that many of its residents are destitute of that urbanity and politeness which should ever be displayed to strangers; but it is probable this circumstances to be attributed chiefly to the pride of nobility and ancestry, which looks down with half averted eyes on supposed inferiority; and to the want of an enlarged commixture with mankind, producing a generosity of disposition, and moderation of principle which are the natural results of extensive commercial pursuits.

Difference of opinion on the actions of public men,—on the measures pursued by persons holding the first political situations in the state, and on religious subjects; are compatible with the purest loyalty and most fervent patriotism, and will be readily acknowledged by those who possess any share of liberality add reflection.

To the infinite credit of Shrewsbury, its population has not been led to the perpetration of any of those acts of violence and atrocity which have disgraced other places, and which are caused by the difference of religious opinion, of the political effervescence of the times in which such outrages may have taken place. This observation, however, is not intended to impute to the inhabitants any thing like a state of passive obedience or wilful ignorance—far otherwise. This judicious conduct by which the welfare and good order of the town have been so essentially promoted, is perhaps rather attributable to the candour and prudence of the leaders of the various political parties, or to the virtue of mutual forbearance happily exercised by the inhabitants at large.

On subjects, however connected with the safety and prosperity of the British Empire, and the welfare of the illustrious house of Brunswick, Shrewsbury has ever been among the foremost in displaying its patriotic spirit and affectionate attachment. The loyalty of the inhabitants has long been pre-eminent, so much so, that it is celebrated by the elegant pen of Shenstone.

> Admir'd Salopia, that with venial pride
>   Eyes her bright form in Severn's ambient wave;
> Fam'd for her cares in loyal perils try'd,
>   HER DAUGHTERS LOVELY AND HER STRIPLINGS
> BRAVE.

As early as the year 1715, this town displayed its consequence and attachment to the present royal family in a very spirited manner. A considerable body of horse and foot was raised by Lord Newport, Sir C. Lloyd, Bart., W. Kynaston, T. Gardner, and J. Fownes, Esquires, for the protection of Shrewsbury; the walls were put in a state of defence, new gates, &c. made, and brigadier Dormer's regiment, then lying in this town, received orders to march to Preston, Shrewsbury being deemed secure from the strength of its *own* garrison. In 1745, also, the earl of Powis raised a regiment here, for the service of the state, into which many gentlemen of the town and neighbourhood entered as volunteers. During the war with the French republic two regiments were raised in Shrewsbury, one by colonel Cuyler, (the present 86th) and the other by colonel, now general Williams, and the inhabitants contributed very liberally towards the crusade against French revolutionary principles.

The maturer efforts of Shrewsbury have not been unworthy the zeal of its youth. When the tocsin of invasion was sounded through the vast dominions of France, and the existence of Britain as an independent nation, was threatened with extinction, the inhabitants of Shrewsbury stepped forward with a noble enthusiasm, in defence of their lives, their liberty and, laws:

> Types of a race, who shall th' invader scorn
>   As rocks resist the billows round their shore:
> Types of a race who shall to time unborn
>   Their country leave unconquer'd as of yore.

A regiment of foot, called the Shrewsbury Volunteers, was formed. It consisted of seven companies of eighty men each, chiefly tradesmen, clothed at an expence of about £3,000, raised by voluntary contribution in the town. Besides this corps, which was commanded by Sir Charles Oakley, Bart., two companies were raised in the town by B. Benyon, and J. Sutton, esq.'s which were attached to that fine regiment the Shropshire Volunteers, under the command of colonel Kynaston Powell, M.P.; and three troops of Cavalry commanded by the honourable William Hill. And had an allwise Providence permitted the invader to set his unhallowed foot on the shores of Britain, there is no doubt but each individual was determined that the spot on which he contended in defence of the noble institutions of his country should have been the throne of his triumph or his grave.

The promptitude with which these associations and others of the same nature throughout the empire, united in the hour of public danger—the fatigues they underwent in acquiring a knowledge of the use of arms—the readiness evinced in the abandonment of their private concerns for the public safety—and the inconveniences and expenses which they incurred on the occasion, surely demanded some other reward than to have their ardour damped by the change in the system of national defence; for to whom in the hour of battle could the protection of their homes and their families, the independence of their country, the sepulchres of their fathers, and the sanctuary of their God, be better entrusted than to those whose courage was animated and strengthened by the most endearing recollections? But such sacrifices, even when the necessity of them was superseded, will not be forgotten—the remembrance of them will live in the minds of their grateful and admiring countrymen, and their services will form a splendid, monument on the page of history.

Nor have the inhabitants been insensible to the miseries attendant on those whose relatives have fallen sacrifices to the heroism and devotion which they displayed during the sanguinary battles of the last twenty years, having very largely contributed to alleviate the wants of their widows and orphans.

The affection and loyalty of the inhabitants of Shrewsbury to their venerable Sovereign was most conspicuously displayed on the National Jubilee, the 25th of October, 1809, the fiftieth anniversary of his Majesty's accession to the crown. On this occasion, liberal subscriptions were entered into for the purpose of discharging the debts of persons in the court of conscience—for relieving the distresses of the sick poor, &c. &c. Joy beamed in every countenance, and gratitude filled every heart. A congratulatory address had been previously voted unanimously, in a general meeting of the inhabitants convened by the mayor.—We give the following abridged account of the celebration of the day from the SHREWSBURY CHRONICLE of October 27:—

> Never, perhaps, has any national occurrence taken place which can afford in retrospect so rich and amiable a gratification as that of Wednesday last. If we contemplate that a general amnesty was proclaimed to all delinquents in our army—that a national banquet was ordered for the brave fellows in our navy—that the prisons in many places were thrown open to the debtors—that there was no such thing, perhaps in the land, as an hungry honest man—and, lastly, that our places of worship were thronged by a people, who, like sons and daughters, had assembled to give thanks to the Almighty for the preservation of the life of their political parent: scarcely could the imagination conceive a happier variety of circumstances from which the mind may derive such sublime enjoyment. How conspicuous on this event has been the attribute of Englishmen—GENEROSITY! And let us also reflect, how much good had been omitted to be done, and how much evil had been produced, if the sums voluntarily subscribed by the people of this kingdom had been squandered in acts of sensuality, and riotous illuminations. Instead of which, the hungry have been filled, the moneyless relieved, and the captive set free.
>
> In deeds of this description, the inhabitants of THIS TOWN have never been deficient. The subscriptions amount to between £400 and £500, and the committee has been indefatigable in proposing, and in executing, the best plans in the distribution of it.
>
> The mode of distribution, fixed upon at a Meeting of the Subscribers, is as follows:—A sum not exceeding 50 Guineas to be applied in the discharge of persons now in the court of conscience, under the direction of a committee.—The like sum to be applied by the same committee in discharging or compounding debts of other poor persons within the town.—A like sum to be applied in the relief of poor sick persons within the town, under the direction of a committee.—The distribution of these sums to take place on or before the 25th of December next.—The Directors of the House of Industry to be recommended to make what addition they shall think proper, on the 25th instant, to the ordinary allowance of

the poor and aged people under their care.—Five Guineas to be given to the ringers; and 7s. to each housekeeper in St. Chad's, St. Mary's, and St. Giles's almshouses.—The remainder given on Tuesday evening (the 24th) to proper persons—one half to St. Chad's parish, and the remaining half in the other four parishes.—Each subscriber to have a right to recommend two persons for each guinea subscribed.

The dawning of Wednesday morning was saluted by ringing of bells; while, from the barges on the Severn, decorated with laurels and flags, which were suspended from their yard-arms and top-masts, the bellowing of cannon was incessantly heard. Shops were closed, and business seemed suspended. At eleven, the mayor and corporation, preceded by their officers, and the wardens and many members of every company of tradesmen, accompanied by their flags and streamers, walked in procession to the church of St. Chad, the band playing God save the King. The sermon was preached by the Rev. Mr. Nunn, from the 11th Nehemiah, 3d verse, "Let the king live for ever;" and the service concluded by singing "God save the King." Sermons were also delivered to crowded congregations at every place of worship in the town. The doors of many of the principal in habitants were ornamented with laurel; at night, fire-works were exhibited from the gardens of Benyon, Esq. and Dr. Evans, and bonfires distinctly descried on the remote eminences of the Wrekin, Haughmond Hill, Grinshill, &c.

We shall conclude by repeating the sentiment, that the future historian, dwelling upon the character of HIS MAJESTY, will, by this day, be released from the trouble of much prolixity. The character of George the Third has been drawn by his people in this spontaneous expression of their sentiments. After a reign of half a century, they rose with one accordant voice, and desired with prayer and praise, with thanks and rejoicings, with deeds of benevolence and charity to all their fellow subjects, to express their gratitude to GOD for having given them so good a King, and for having spared his life so long.

One remark will surely occur to every person who reads this and other accounts of the universal spirit that has pervaded the bosoms of Englishmen on this occasion:—If the strength of a state center in the virtue of its people; the virtue of a people in affection for their sovereign, and a reciprocal love, link both together, then is England powerful indeed! 'What shall subdue this spirit?'

Description of the Town.

PUBLIC BUILDINGS.

IN entering on our general description of the town, its public buildings naturally claim the first share of attention. They will be found classed under the heads of Public, Religious, and Charitable erections, and noticed under that order: and whether we consider them in the accommodation which they present for the transaction of the business respectively carried on in them, for the antiquity of some, or for the elegance of their erection, they will no doubt prove sources of recreation to, and well worthy the inspection of, the stranger.

The Castle

Is supposed to have been founded by Roger de Montgomery, about the year 1068. It continued in his family until the reign of Henry I, when by the rebellion of earl Robert de Belesme it was forfeited to the king, who committed the care of it to a constable, usually the sheriff, it being then extremely useful for the defence of the adjacent country.

This ancient fortress is built of red stone, on the N.E. part of the isthmus on which the town stands, and being erected on a commanding eminence, was admirably calculated to "roll back the tide of war" and to defend Shrewsbury from the frequent incursions of the neighbouring Welsh, who were continually devastating the surrounding country. When the incorporation of the principality with the English dominions took place, it ceased to enjoy the importance which its situation on the Welsh border had previously given to it; and after experiencing a variety of changes in its masters, it was granted by Charles II. to lord Newport, afterwards earl of Bradford; since which period it became the property of the late venerable sir William Pulteney, bart. who greatly repaired and rendered it a comfortable residence. Sir William at his death bequeathed it to the right honourable the earl of Darlington, its present possessor.

The history of the Town and the Castle are so intimately connected, that we shall content ourselves with giving a brief description of its ancient and present appearance. According to Leland, it was fast hastening to decay in the reign of Henry VIII. and indeed it has suffered so much from the ravages of time, rather than from those of war, that it is doubtful what idea to form of its original size; but it is at least probable, when its importance as a border fortress is considered, that it occupied a much larger space than that marked out by its existing walls.

The only buildings remaining are the keep, the walls of the inner court, and the great arch of the interior gate; they are built of red stone, and the former has been converted into a commodious and pleasant dwelling, and is at present occupied by J. C. Pelham, esq. It consists of two round towers of equal diameter, embattled and pierced, connected by a square building about 100 feet in length and about the same in height, in which are many spacious and excellent rooms. At the entrance, which opens on a newly-erected grand staircase, is a statue of Roger de Montgomery. The arch of the gateway is about 18 feet high, semicircular, and with plain round facings. Its walls appear to have sustained a tower, from whence hung the portcullis. The area of the court has latterly been cleared of its buildings, and is now formed into a beautiful garden. On the circular grass-plot in front of the castle, the newly-elected knights of the shire are girt with their swords by the sheriff, which, as it is an ancient custom, is still permitted, although the castle and its grounds are private property.

In the south corner of this court is a lofty mount, on which is erected a watch tower, now converted into a pleasant summer room, from which is commanded a grand and diversified prospect of uncommon richness and beauty. The mount, rising abruptly from the margin of the Severn, crowned with its venerable tower, its bold and abrupt bank being richly clothed with the foliage of various species of trees and skirted by the majestic stream which rolls at its base, has also, when viewed from a distance, a beautiful and picturesque appearance. Shrewsbury, though the most important station on the Welsh border, and though frequently thrown into possession of its enemies, never sustained more than two sieges. Its natural and artificial strength might probably deter an adverse army from investing it in a regular way, for it was protected not only by its castle, but by

Walls,

fenced with towers which completely surrounded it.

The first stone rampart extended only across the isthmus to the river on each side, and was raised by Robert de Belesme. In the reign of Henry III. the inhabitants of this place having suffered greatly during the rebellion of the earl of Pembroke, were exhorted to secure themselves by building a wall entirely round the town, which, by the aid of the royal bounty, was accomplished in 32 years. An additional rampart, by order of Oliver Cromwell, was constructed, as it is said, from the materials of Shrawardine castle, and extended from the wall of earl Robert at the river's brink to the Welsh bridge: though now ruinous it forms a tolerable connecting path between the northern and western ends of the town.—Of the old ramparts, those on the northern and eastern sides of the town have long since disappeared; their foundations, which are easy to be traced, form the groundwork of modern houses. On the south, a considerable portion remains, and part of it is kept in repair as a public walk; but it retains little of its original appearance, having been considerably lowered, and entirely stripped of its battlements. The towers have been all taken down except one, which stands on this wall, between the bottom of Swan Hill and Belmont. It is square and embattled, and has two stories, the entrance of the higher being from the top of the wall, through a small pointed arch, which does not appear of older date than the time of Henry IV. The town, according to Leland, who beheld its fortifications entire, was more than a mile in compass; which extent may probably be a third more in modern computation. There were formerly three principal

Gates

to Shrewsbury; one near the Castle called the North Gate, and one on each of the bridges; that on the east called the Abbey Gate, and that on the west the Welsh Gate. A part of the southern tower of the north gate is the only remain of these once formidable fortifications.

The Town Hall

Is situated in High Street, and was erected in 1785 from a design by Mr. Haycock of this town, at an expense of £11,000, which was raised by a county rate.

It is an elegant structure of free stone, presenting a handsome front to the street. On the front of the pediment, which is supported by four lofty columns of the Ionic order, is a fine figure of Justice in *bas relief*, seated on a rock, beneath which, over the centre door, are the arms of the town handsomely ornamented with appropriate emblems.

The ground floor consists of a vestibule and two courts, in which the assizes for the county are held. Under the one appropriated to the crown bar, is a cell, for the reception of prisoners. A beautiful spiral stone staircase leads to the higher story, where is a large room intended for county meetings, one for the use of the grand jury of the county, with record and other offices for the use of the county and town.

The grand jury room is decorated with portraits of George I. given by Mr. Edward Elisha; of George II. given by Thomas Wingfield, esq.; of George III. and queen Charlotte, given by sir Thomas Jones, bart.; and one of the gallant and celebrated admiral Benbow, given by his sister, Mrs. Elizabeth Hind.

Immediately adjoining is

The Market House.

From an inscription over the northern arch it appears that

> "The XVth day of June was this building begun, William Jones and Thomas Charlton, Gent. then Bailiffs, and was erected and covered in their time 1595."

It is built entirely of free stone, and is one of the largest of similar erections in the kingdom. In the centre of the principal front, which faces the west, is a spacious portal, over which are the arms of queen Elizabeth in high relief. Attached to the imposts of the great arch are pillars, supporting each the figure of a lion bearing a shield on its breast. Above are two stories, with large square mullioned windows. On each side this portal is an open arcade, consisting of three spacious round arches, which form the main building, over which is a range of square windows with mullions, and a very rich parapet, consisting of a series of embrazures carved like the Ionic volute, between which at alternate distances, are a kind of grotesque pinnacles in the same style. At the north and south ends are large open arches, the whole edifice being finished above by sharp pointed gables.

The ground floor of this building is appropriated to the corn market, and is 105 feet long by 24 feet wide. A room over of similar size was formerly rented by the company of drapers, and used by them for a flannel market on Thursdays; but the sale of that staple article of Welsh manufacture having been removed to Welsh Pool, it has been rented of late as an ironmonger's warehouse. Over the northern arch is placed the statue of Richard duke of York, removed hence from the old bridge in 1791, as appears by the inscription at his right hand: on his left are the arms of the town finely sculptured in relief.

Its spacious area is a useful promenade for the inhabitants in bad weather, and its architecture is a fine specimen of the fantastic style of the 16th century.

Lord Hill's Column.

The splendid achievements of the British army in Spain and Portugal from 1808 to 1814, together with the disastrous retreat of Napoleon from his Russian campaign, and the subsequent occupation of France by the allied troops, having produced a general peace, a proposition appeared in the Shrewsbury Chronicle of December the 17th, 1813, by the Proprietor of that paper, to erect some suitable memorial of the prominent part lord Hill had acted throughout the whole of those eventful campaigns.—At a meeting in the News Room on the following day, nearly £400 was subscribed to carry this intention into effect. Subsequently, however, it was determined to extend the original plan, a meeting of the inhabitants of the town was called, and it was resolved to solicit subscriptions generally from all who participated in the triumphs of their country, or who felt any respect for the brilliant and varied services of the gallant general.

After a variety of plans had been proposed it was at length determined to erect the column now under notice. The first stone was laid on the 27th of December, 1814, agreeably to masonic rule, by Richard Phillips, esq. master of the Salopian Lodge, and at that time mayor of Shrewsbury. The foundation stone, which weighed four tons and a half, is of the following dimensions, viz: length 11 feet 3 inches, breadth 3 feet, and 2 feet thick. In a cavity underneath, a bottle was deposited, containing gold and silver coins of George III. accompanied with the SHREWSBURY CHRONICLE of the preceding Friday. Over the cavity was a plate bearing the following

INSCRIPTION

Of this Column, intended to be erected to commemorate the brilliant achievements of Lieutenant-General ROWLAND LORD HILL, Knight of the Bath, and Knight of the Tower and Sword.

The first Stone was laid by RICHARD PHILLIPS, Esquire, Mayor of Shrewsbury, and Matter of the Salopian Lodge of free and accepted Masons, assisted by the Chaplain, Wardens, the Brethren of this and Deputies from other Lodges, upon the 27th Day of December, in the year of our Lord, 1814, and in the year of Masonry—5814, being the *Festival of St. John*. The funds for this beautiful Memorial, in honour of splendid talent and private worth, were furnished by a public Subscription, raised chiefly by the inhabitants of the town and county of Salop.

The column is situated on a rising ground, at the entrance of this town from the London and Bath roads. From its insulated and lofty situation, it is seen from many parts of the town, and is conspicuous at a considerable distance in the country.

	FT.	IN.
The height of the pedestal is	13	0
shaft and capital	91	6
pedestal supporting the statue	11	6
statue	16	0

| The whole height | 132 | 6 |

Solidity and durability have been particularly attended to in its construction, the stones with which it has been built, being as large as could conveniently be raised, from an excellent quarry at Grinshill, in the neighbourhood of Shrewsbury.

The pedestal is square, standing upon two steps, having a large pier or buttress at each angle, upon which are placed Lions couchant. The piers are formed of three stones in each, the top one of each on which the lions are placed, being 10 feet 6 inches long, 4 feet 3 inches wide, and 3 feet 3 inches deep, and their weight 10 tons. The lower diameter of the column is 15 feet, and the masonry 2 feet 3 inches in thickness; the top diameter 10 feet 6 inches, by 1 foot 6 inches in thickness. Each course of stones is 3 feet high, six stones form the course. There are 326 stones in the whole structure, and the top stone immediately under the statue, weighs two and a half tons. There are 17,993 cubic feet in the whole, and its weight is 1120 tons. There is a beautiful staircase up the shaft, the view of the surrounding country from the top, being most extensive. The expense was about £5,500.

The proportion of this column is half a diameter higher than those in the portico of the celebrated Parthenon at Athens, and is THE LARGEST GREEK DORIC COLUMN IN THE WORLD. The figure is designed and executed by Messrs. Coade and Sealy, of London, in their artificial stone, which is so well calculated to resist the action of the weather. The lions are worked in Grinshill stone, by Mr. Carline of this place. The contractors were the late Mr. Simpson, and Mr. Lawrence: owing to the death of the former the contract devolved upon his successor Mr. Straphen. The original design is by Mr. Edward Haycock, architect, of this town, with some alterations in the pedestal by Mr. Harrison, of Chester.

The Town & County Goal.

This building, a pleasant and admirably constructed brick edifice, was finished in 1793, at the expense of about £30,000, on a plan furnished by Mr. Haycock, architect, of this town. It was erected in consequence of the light diffused on the subject of prisons by the later philanthropic Mr. Howard, the old gaol being (says Mr. Howard) "both wretched in its accommodations, and a complete school of vice."

The prison is situate on the banks of the river, on a dry gravelly soil on the south-east side of the town, in the immediate vicinity of the castle, and is spacious, airy, well supplied with water, and as comfortable as these abodes of human misfortune and depravity possibly can be.

The entrance is through a free stone gateway, having a lodge on each side, over the arch of which is a fine bust of Howard, presented by the late Rowland Hunt, and Thomas Knight, esquires, two county magistrates. There are reception cells in the lodges for the examination of the persons by the surgeon previous to their being lodged in the different apartments; during their continuance in the prison, criminals wear a woollen jacket, waistcoat and cap, composed of blue and yellow stripes before conviction, after which the dress is changed for one of brown and yellow. All executions take place on the flat roof of the northern lodge, when all the criminals are brought into the area before the governor's house to witness the awful scene. This house, in which is an apartment for the magistrates, faces the entrance gate, in the centre of the west front of the prison. The chapel, which is a neat octagonal structure, well calculated for the important purposes of its erection, stands in the centre of the whole building, and is so arranged that every class of prisoners is separated and hid from each other, though all may see the officiating clergyman. The prison, the boundary wall of which encloses two acres of ground, and is 16 feet high, is divided into four principal courts, besides smaller ones, and not only are the sexes separated, but each description of prisoners are subdivided, into classes, which have each their respective courts and day rooms. The debtor's rooms are airy and comfortable, commanding many pleasing views of the adjacent country. At the eastern extremity is the infirmary, near which the under keeper resides, who has constantly for sale various articles manufactured by the prisoners, the profits of which are applied for their benefit.

Closely allied to the superior construction of the prison are the excellent and judicious regulations for its internal management, which, whilst they tend to ameliorate the condition of the unhappy sufferers, are calculated to reclaim their vicious habits; and should they return to the bosom of society, stimulate them to atone for their depredations on their fellow-creatures, by their honest and exemplary deportment in future. Prayers are read every Thursday, and a sermon preached every Sunday by the chaplain, and the justices appointed at the quarter sessions visit the different apartments of the prison when they please, and have the power of making any alteration in the mode of treating the criminals which to them may appear judicious.

Convinced that the design of punishment is to prevent the commission of crimes, and to repair the injury that has thereby been done to society or the individual, and that it is the duty of every good government to *reform* rather than *exterminate* offenders, the exertions of the late Rowland Hunt, esq. were directed to the formation of the following excellent plan, which was instituted in 1797.

First—To enable debtors to gain a livelihood while in confinement; to reward their industry and good behaviour while there; and to furnish them with some implements or materials on quitting prison, the better to support themselves and their families on their return to society.

Secondly—To encourage industry, penitence, and orderly behaviour in criminal prisoners; and to furnish with clothes and implements those who on quitting prison receive a certificate of good behaviour.

Thirdly—To provide all those who are dismissed, with a small sum for immediate maintenance, to prevent the great temptation of committing a crime for that purpose.

This praiseworthy charity, the subscriptions to which from the county at large amount to about £80 yearly; also distributes bibles and prayer books to the wretched objects of its bounty, and thus endeavours to impress on the minds of these outcasts of society, the sacred lessons of divine wisdom. The benevolent stranger will perceive in the large outer gate of the prison, two small apertures, and on the other side two boxes are affixed, into one of which he may drop his mite, "to prisoners in a state of reformation," and in the other "to debtors in a state of industry."

The Military Depot,

Is a very handsome brick edifice, erected by government in the year 1806, from a design by Mr. Wyatt, at an expense of about £10,000. It stands in a piece of ground near St. Giles's Church, at the east end of the Abbeyforegate.

The principal building is 135 feet by 39, in two stories, and is capable of containing 25,000 stand of arms. Within the enclosure are two magazines for ammunition, and a small neat house at each angle for the storekeeper, armourer, and subalterns' guard.—It was intended for the reception of the arms of the volunteer corps of Shropshire and the adjoining counties, but until lately very few arms of any description have been deposited here—in fact it has been a complete sinecure. Mr. Linton is the present governor.

The English, or East Bridge,

Called also the Stone Bridge, which connects the suburb of Abbey-foregate with the town, was finished in 1774, from a plan produced by Mr. Gwyn, at an expense of £16,000 raised by public subscription. This bridge, which is 400 feet in length, is built of Grinshill free stone, on seven semicircular arches, and crowned with a fine balustrade. The central arch is 60 feet in width, and 40 in height from the bed of the river, the two arches at the extremities being 35 feet wide and 20 high. The breadth between the balustrades is 20 feet.—On the northern front is the head of Sabrina in bas relief and the date of its erection. Its ornaments are tasteful, and it may justly be classed among the most elegant modern erections in the empire. Some persons, probably, may conceive that the elevation of the centre is too great, but when they are informed that in the memorable flood of 1795, even the great arch was not more than capacious enough to admit the torrent, they will no doubt be inclined to praise rather than censure the artist, who was actuated by a desire to blend the useful with the ornamental.

The Welsh Bridge,

Built in the opposite direction to the before named structure, and which received its name as being the grand route into Wales, was finished in 1795, from a design by Messrs. Tilly and Carline of this place. It consists of five spacious arches with balustrades above, and is 266 feet in length, with a driving road 20 feet wide, and paved on each side, for the convenience of foot passengers, 5 feet. It is a plain though neat erection, and has a remarkably solid and substantial appearance.

Public Subscription Library,

Situated on St. John's Hill, is a plain brick edifice, formerly a private house, and has been lately purchased by the Committee of the above institution, and fitted up for the purpose of lodging the books belonging to the Society. The number of subscribers is about 140, who pay annually £1. 11s. 6d. and 2 guineas entrance; but their shares are transferable. The managers of the society are a president, a treasurer, a committee of twelve, who sit gratuitously, and a librarian at a stipend. The following are some of the principal laws and regulations:—The library is open for the free use of subscribers five hours every day at the rooms, with the right of having several books at one time at their own houses, a certain number of days. Forfeits are established and rigorously enforced for detaining and damaging of books.—The method of admitting books is, for any member to write down the title, size and price at the library, with his signature, one clear week before the monthly meeting, at which period it will be ordered, if the majority of the subscribers present are agreeable.

The society which has been instituted about forty years, now possesses 5000 volumes—a valuable mass of general literature in every department. Neither divinity nor law has been permitted to *load* the shelves; and in the matter of that great stumbling block of mixed associations, *politics*, a due regard to that invaluable maxim "audi alteram partem," has never been forgot or violated, and diversity of opinion has only promoted the successful progress of the establishment.

Subscription Coffee Room

Is attached to the county-hall, and is supplied with several London and provincial papers.

Chronicle News-Room.

This is situate on St. John's Hill, and forms part of the Library House. It is furnished not only with a very extensive variety of London and Provincial Newspapers and the Gazette, but also with Reviews, Magazine, Army and Navy Lists, and the best Pamphlets of the day, &c.

To each of these institutions strangers are admitted on being introduced by a subscriber.

Beside these institutions there are several private READING SOCIETIES in the town.

New Church of St. Chad.

This church, situated near that beautiful promenade the Quarry, is erected in a style highly ornamental, from a design by Mr. Stuart, an architect from London. The admirable execution of the masonry, and the beauty of the stone, have an extremely elegant appearance. The first stone was laid on the 2d of March, 1790, and the building was consecrated on the 28th of August, 1792. The body of the church is a rotunda, 100 feet in diameter, having a fine steeple at its south-east end. In the steeple is an octagonal belfry, containing a melodious peal of twelve bells, surmounted by a small dome, supported on eight Corinthian pillars.

The principal entrance is through the large door under the steeple, to the lower division of which is attached a portico, elevated on a flight of steps, and supported by four Doric columns. The interior has a rich and noble appearance, especially since its recent painting, which in some measure has corrected that light and theatrical effect hitherto complained of. The gallery which encircles the whole of the church, except the chancel, is supported by a double circular range of short pillars with Ionic capitals. From its front rises a series of columns which support the roof, intended to imitate the Corinthian order. The chancel is separated from the church by two insulated Corinthian-columns, with highly enriched architraves. Beside the usual appendages of a chancel, the Creed, Commandments, and Lord's Prayer—a fine painted window, executed by Eginton, and removed here from Lichfield cathedral, was erected in the large window, in 1807, at the expense of the parishioners.—The subject is the resurrection of our Saviour, from a design by West. In the gallery is a good organ.

Notwithstanding the objections which have been made to the architectural plan of this church, it is possessed of one advantage, which, it is presumed tends to obviate all of them, namely convenient accommodation for a congregation of 2000 persons, which should be the object principally kept in view in all similar erections. It was built at an expense of about £18,000: £15,000 of which remains as a debt, on the church at this period.

The patron of the living is the king—the present vicar, the Rev. Thomas Stedman, M.A. Organist Mr. John Wynne.

From the dome of this church there is a most beautiful panoramic view of the town, and a very extensive range of the fertile plain of Shropshire.

The Abbey of St. Peter & St. Paul.

The present church once formed part of a magnificent and richly endowed abbey, founded by Roger de Montgomery, soon after the Norman conquest. Here that powerful baron, in the decline of his life, retired, relinquishing his warlike habits for the severities of the Benedictine monks, and adopting the custom mentioned by Milton, of those

> who, to be sure of Paradise,
> Dying, put on the weeds of Dominic,
> Or in Franciscan think to pass disguised.

Originally it was of very considerable extent, comprehending within its enclosure nearly nine acres, now used as gardens and pleasure grounds to the adjoining mansions, together with a spacious fish-pond.

This once celebrated structure, in common with others similar in their institution, suffered considerable dilapidations in the reign of Henry the eighth. In consequence of this and the mouldering waste of time, a small portion only remains, and what does exist has been cruelly mutilated in its repairs; its nave, western tower and northern porch, being the only fragments left to tell the history of its pristine magnificence and grandeur.

The tower is a finely proportioned structure; its portal has a round Norman arch deeply recessed, and another of a pointed form, inserted within it at some subsequent period. Above this is one of the noblest windows in the kingdom, its height being 46 feet by 22 feet wide. It is divided by its mulliens into seven "days", or compartments below, of which there are two tiers, and its arched head is sharp pointed, and filled with a profusion of the most delicate tracery. On each side is a mouldering nich, in one of which was a statue of St. Peter, and in the other St. Paul. Between the double bell windows in front, is the figure of an armed knight within a nich, supposed from its surrounding decorations and ornaments, to represent that celebrated warrior, Edward III. The tower contains eight bells. Within the arch which once led to the south wing of the transept, is an ancient figure clad in mail, supposed by some, to be intended to perpetuate the memory of earl Roger, the munificent patron of the abbey, and to this effect an inscription was placed within the tomb, by the heralds at their visitation of this county, in 1633. Others suppose it to belong to some other warrior of subsequent times, monuments of this description not being known at such an early period.

The ravages which this venerable pile has suffered are, perhaps, more strikingly visible in its interior than its exterior; but it still presents a solemn and majestic appearance, and whilst it proudly reminds us of its ancient grandeur, awfully forewarns us of "another and a better world."—The altar-piece is in the style of the last century, with paintings of Moses and Aaron, and finishes the east end.

There are several monuments and inscriptions in memory of the Prynces, Baldwins, Reckes, and many other ancient and respectable Salopian families. The armorial bearings in the great west window, were restored A.D. 1815, from an ancient drawing in the Herald's Office. The east window is also adorned with painted glass. In the center compartment, under gothic canopies, are large figures of St. Peter and St. Paul, with their appropriate symbols; above are the arms of England, the see of Lichfield, the Founder of the Abbey, and of Lord Berwick, the munificent donor of the window; on each side are escutcheons of the vicars from the year 1500. The bones of St. Winyfred were deposited in this abbey with great splendour, in the reign of Stephen.

The organ and the handsome gothic screen on which it stands, were erected in 1806. It is a very fine instrument, made by Mr. Gray, of London, and cost 365 guineas. On the screen are the arms of the principal benefactors.

In the parish chest are two small oval seals exactly similar in their dimensions, impresses and legends. Two clothed arms issue from the opposite sides of the area, one bearing a crosier, the other a naked sword; in the centre, a wand or staff of office. Inscription, "Sigillum commune de Fforyate Monachor"—the common seal of Monks Foregate. Some of our most skilful antiquaries are unable to give a sufficient reason why Monks Foregate came to have a common seal. Some of them have supposed that the parish might have obtained a charter of incorporation, while others think that it might have been assumed without authority. Neither of the two seals appear much older than the 15th century.

The patron of the living is Lord Berwick—the Rev. H. Burton, vicar, and Mr. John Amott, organist.

But the remain of this abbey which has most excited the attention of antiquaries, is a beautiful little structure on the south side of the gardens. Its plan is octagon, 6 feet in diameter. Some broken steps which did not belong to it originally, lead through a narrow flat arched door on the east, to the inside. The south part stands on a fragment of the ruins. The corresponding side projects considerably from the wall, resting upon a single corbel, terminating in a head. From this point it gradually swells, bound with a multitude of delicate ribbed mouldings, until it forms the basement under the floor. An obtuse dome of stone is suspended over the whole, at about eight feet from the base, supported on six narrow pointed arches, rising from pillars similar to the mullions of the windows. One of the remaining sides of the octagon is a solid blank wall, and in the other is a door. The roof within is vaulted on eight ribs, which spring from the wall immediately under the cavity of the dome. At their crossing in the centre is a boss, bearing a representation of the crucifixion, considerably relieved. The spaces between the divisions of the three northern arches, four feet above the bottom, are filled up with stone pannels, over which they are entirely open, a circumstance which, by permitting the light, is productive of a beautiful effect. On the centre pannel are two small figures in elegant tabernacles; in one of these is the figure of an angel, in the other, that of a woman, whom he is addressing; the whole seems intended to represent the annunciation. The right hand pannel is embellished with images of St. Peter and St. Paul bearing their respective symbols, with similar enrichments, and that on the left has two figures in monastic habits, one of them a female, probably St. Winyfred, the other a monk; the height of every figure is eighteen inches. The arches on the southern side are without ornaments, and are now quite open two feet from the floor.

In forming a garden on the site of the Abbey Cloisters, a great variety of fragments were met with, consisting of painted tiles with various devices, rich gothic tracery, window mullions, &c. and a very beautiful part of the pavement of the refectory; this, from its situation, being about 23 feet from the line of the outer refectory wall, and being part of the border of a pavement, satisfactorily proves the use to which this beautiful Gothic pulpit was applied, it being a custom in Benedictine monasteries, for one monk to read to the others during their meals in the refectory. In a parallel line, and at 12 feet distance from the wall of the dormitory, a considerable number of small Norman capitals and bases were found, strongly bedded in cement, and forming a foundation to some superstructure. As the west side of the cloisters must have occupied this situation, it may be presumed that there were cloisters of more ancient architecture, than these destroyed at the Reformation, to which the fragments found in the garden belonged.

St. Marys Church.

This venerable church is situated on a parallel with Castle-street, at the north-east part of the town, in a small area; and with the exception of St. Giles', is the only structure of this place, which has been handed down to the present time in an entire state. It is built in the form of a cross, consisting of a nave side isles, transept, choir and its chapels, with a west steeple. The exterior presents various styles of ancient architecture. The basement of the tower is of red stone, and contains the small round-headed windows of the early Norman era. From the bell story the pointed style takes place, and is of the grey free stone of Grinshill quarry, as is also the greatest part of the fabric. The tower is large, but low. The upper story has on every side handsome double windows. From the tower rises a lofty and beautiful spire. The windows of the lower parts bear the remains of rich spiring canopies and pinnacles. The height of the tower is 76 feet, of the spire 140.

Upon the south side of the church is a stone porch of early Norman architecture. Its outward arch is circular, with diagonal or zig-zag mouldings, the inner rib obtusely pointed. The small pointed windows on each side are curious specimens of the very earliest rudiments of the mullioned window. The ceiling also presents an example of the most ancient kind of groined vault, and consists of four round massive ribs crossing each other in the centre, without any boss or ornament. The semicircular arch of the interior door is a good specimen of the style of building in fashion from the conquest to the days of Henry II. The north door is an elegant example of this ancient kind of building. Formerly it was an unsightly wooden porch, which was removed in 1801. The arches of the north and south doors of the transept are in the same early style. The decorations of the latter are rather uncommon, having lozenge pannels placed alternately, and each filled with an embossed flower. The side aisles, with the upper story of the nave and choir, have pointed windows with mullions, while those of the transept are long and lancet shaped, without any. The higher walls of the nave were, in the repair of 1786, very injudiciously raised some feet above their original level, which altogether destroys the ancient proportions, and gives the whole building a top-heavy appearance. Formerly the church was crowned with pinnacles, which issued from the spaces between each window and the corner buttresses of the transept and choir, but now, excepting those on the chapel, not one remains.

Within, the church is spacious, lofty, interesting, and from its venerable and solemn appearance, admirably adapted to the purposes of religious meditation.

> As chanced, the portal of the sacred pile
> Stood open, and we entered. On my frame,
> At such transition from the fervid air,
> A grateful coolness fell, that seem'd to strike
> The heart, in concert with that temperate awe
> And natural reverence which the place inspired.
>
> WORDSWORTH.

The walls of the nave are supported on each side by four semicircular arches, with moulding peculiar to the pointed style, and these spring from finely clustered pillars, their shafts having the small flat rib which belongs to the 13th century. The capitals are highly enriched with foliage, and, as is usual in ancient churches, are all of different designs. Above the arches is a clere-story, with a high range of short windows on both sides, running the whole length of the church. These are irregularly ranged in couplets, and have heads very obtusely pointed, each divided by a single mullion. The ceiling of the nave, which is of oak, rises into an extremely flat arch, separated by its principal beams into square pannels, including circles richly adorned with quatrefoils and foliage. The ribs and bosses at their intersections, are carved, with double roses, devices and knots; those attached to the centre beam having pendant ornaments, pelicans, angels with musical instruments, and grotesque sculptures. The chancel is considerably elevated by two ascents of steps. On each side is a pointed arch, blocked up, resting upon imposts similar to the clustered pillars in the nave. Several

> — marble monuments are here displayed
> Upon the walls: and on the floor beneath
> Sepulchral stones appear, with emblems graven
> And foot-worn epitaphs, and some with small
> And shining effigies of brass inlaid,

belonging to the Lyster, Morhall, Lloyd, Gardner, and Sandford families. On the north side, near the altar, is a beautiful triple window, with arches remarkably sharp pointed, the centre rising much higher than those of each side and supported upon slender insulated columns, whose capitals are adorned with foliage, busts, and grotesque heads. The ceiling of oak pannelling, was in this part quite plain. The interstices between the beams have been plastered over and painted with trefoil and other appropriate enrichments, and the intersections adorned with carved roses and devices, collected from the ruins of St. Chad's and St. Alkmond's. In the chancel, is an altar tomb, upon which is a recumbent figure of a cross legged knight, in linked armour, the sides adorned with rich foliated niches, once containing figures. This monument is supposed to belong to John de Leyborne, of Berwick Leyborne, last of the family. In the vestry, under a low pointed arch, is a plain altar tomb, which has formerly been ornamented with shields; on the massy alabaster slab which covers it, are engraven the figures of a man in armour, bareheaded, with his wife, both in the act of prayer. From the inscription which is somewhat defaced, we learn, that it was erected to — Stafford and Catherine his wife, in 1463. In the transept and nave there are some singular monumental figures, brought here from the ruins of St. Chad's and St. Alkmond's, but to whom they belonged has not been ascertained.

The lower divisions of the great window which terminates the chancel, is occupied by some ancient painted glass brought from old St. Chad's, representing the root of Jesse: the arch or head is made up with ancient coats of arms and modern stained glass. The altar piece is a rich Grecian design. The altar is a fine slab of Sienna marble bordered with jasper, and was the gift of the Rev. Hugh Owen, vicar of St. Julian's, when curate here in 1789. In the gallery at the west end of the nave, is a very handsome organ, made by John Harris and John Byfield, and as this church, with the exception of St. Lawrence, at Ludlow, is the handsomest in the county, so the organ with a like exception, is the most powerful and best toned. In the tower is a musical peal of ten bells, the harmony of which is not exceeded by that of any other peal in the town.

On the south-west side of the church-yard is a tomb-stone erected to the memory of Thomas Anderson, a lieutenant in Ligonier's regiment of light horse, who was tried at Worcester for desertion, in the first German war of George II. and removed here for execution. He was shot on Kingsland, near this town, on the 11th of December, 1752, and met his fate with calmness and fortitude. At the foot of the tower is a stone in memory of Robert Cadman, who in January, 1740, in an attempt to descend from the top of the spire by means of a rope affixed to it, the other end of which was placed in the fields on the opposite side of the river, fell lifeless in St. Mary's Friars, through the breaking of the rope, amidst an immense number of spectators. The inscription is quaint:—

> Let this small monument record the name
> Of Cadman, and to future times proclaim,
> How from a bold attempt to fly from this high spire,
> Across the Sabrine stream, he did acquire
> His fatal end: 'Twas not for want of skill
> Or courage to perform the task, he fell,
> No, no, a faulty cord being drawn too tight,
> Hurried his soul on high to take her flight,
> Which bid the body here beneath, good night.

The right of presentation to this living is vested in the Corporation of Shrewsbury at large; and in the choice of a minister, (who must at least be a M.A.) the son of a burgess who has been brought up at the Free Schools; or one born in the parish of Chirbury, is to have the preference. The church is a royal peculiar, the Official having cognizance of all ecclesiastical matters arising within the parish and its subordinate chapelries. He is stiled "Ordinary and Official, Principal of the peculiar and exempt jurisdiction of the Free Royal Chapel of the Blessed Virgin Mary." The present minister, who is also official, is the Rev. John Brickdale Blakeway, M.A.—Organist, Mr. Thomas Tomlins.

St. Julian's Church,

Situated at the top of Wyle Cop, originally of Saxon election, is a plain substantial structure of brick and stone, rebuilt in 1750, at an expense of

£2000. At the west end is the square tower of the old church; the lower part being of red stone and in a more ancient style than the higher story, which is of the 16th century. It is furnished with six bells. In the east wall of the chancel is a small female figure within a foliated tabernacle, preserved from the reins of the old church, and probably representing St. Juliana, the patroness.

The form of this church is an oblong square, 83ft. by 48ft. the roof being supported by four Doric columns on each side. The ceiling is ornamented with the fret work of the old church. The altar-piece is adorned with Ionic pilasters, supporting a rich cornice and architrave. The east window is filled with fine painted glass, consisting chiefly of a large ancient figure of St. James, bearing the Scriptures in his hand, purchased in 1804, from the splendid collection of glass brought from Rouen, in Normandy, during the French Revolution, and is extremely well executed. Above the Apostle are escutcheons of the arms of France and England, quarterly, and those of the corporation, and see of Lichfield. The arms of the present and ancient patrons of the church, Earl Tankerville, Sir John Astley, and Prince, together with those of the families of Rocke, Powys, Bowdler, &c. &c. are exhibited in various situations in the edifice, which is likewise beautified with a variety of painted and stained glass. The only ancient monument in this church which is worthy the attention of the antiquarian, is a slab of coarse alabaster, lately removed from the church-yard into the chancel. It is nearly a foot in thickness and as hard as flint; and besides a modern epitaph which has been inserted in the centre of it, it contains round the edge this inscription, in Longobardic capitals, now nearly obliterated, but capable of being read, EASMONYND TROVMWYN GIST ICI DIEV DE SA ALME EN EYT MERCI AMEN. i.e. Edmund Trowmwyn lieth here, may God have mercy on his soul. Amen.

There is an organ in the gallery.

The Earl of Tankerville is the patron. The present incumbent is the Rev. Hugh Owen, F.A.S. Archdeacon of Salop, portionary of Bampton, Oxfordshire, and prebendary of Salisbury.

Old St. Chad's Church

Is situated at the top of Belmont.

This once venerable pile was founded previous to the Norman conquest, by one of the kings of Mercia, soon after the expulsion of the Britons, on a site of a palace belonging to one of the princes of Powis, which was destroyed during the wars between the Britons and their Saxon invaders. In 1393, a considerable part of the structure was burnt down through the carelessness of a plumber, then repairing the lead on the roof, who, frightened at beholding the edifice in flames, endeavoured to escape over the ford of the Severn, near the eastern gate, but was drowned in the attempt. In the early part of the year 1788, the church was observed to be decaying fast, and a respectable architect, who was employed to survey it, advised that the tower should be taken down, in order to relieve the mouldering pillars of their vast weight. Unfortunately, this salutary advice was not acted upon; in lieu thereof, partial repairs were undertaken, and the attempt to remove a shattered pillar, that a firmer one might be erected in its place, completed its ruin. On the second day after the workmen had commenced their destructive operations, the decayed pillar gave way, and in consequence, the tower fell about four o'clock the following morning, July 9, 1788, on the roof of the church, and overwhelmed the greater part of the sacred edifice in ruinous desolation.

About a month previous to this occurrence, the church had been thronged with thousands, who had assembled to witness the interment of an officer with military honours.

Although a considerable part of old building remained, it was not deemed advisable to rebuild the church on its ancient site. The present fragment of it, which was formerly the Bishop's chancel, was fitted up for the purpose of performing the rites of sepulture in, and at this time it is used as a charity school.

It is worthy of remark, that the light of the reformation first dawned in Shrewsbury in this church.

St. Alkmond's Church,

Situate immediately adjoining St. Julian's, was originally founded by Elfrida, daughter of Offa, king of Mercia; and like some others in Shrewsbury, was erected at different periods and in different styles of architecture in the form of a cross. At the destruction of St. Chad's church, the parishioners, alarmed for the safety of their ancient structure, caused it to be thoroughly examined, and in consequence of some symptoms of decay exhibited in the roof, they determined on the demolition of the old church and the erection of a new one on a part of its site. The present building was accordingly opened for divine worship in November, 1795, at an expence of about £3000, one half of which might have been saved by a judicious repair of the original erection, and thus preserved for ages. The beautiful spire-steeple at the west end, is the only part which escaped the general devastation. It is 184 feet in height, and is highly ornamental to the town, especially when seen from the adjacent country. It contains a musical peal of eight bells.

The plan of the church is an oblong square, 84 feet by 44, with a small recess for the altar, over which is a handsome painted window, by Eginton; the subject is emblematical of Faith, kneeling on a cross, with the eyes elevated and arms extended towards a celestial crown which appears amidst the opening clouds. "Be faithful unto death, and I will give thee a crown of life," is the motto.

Previous to the demolition of the old church, there were a variety of ancient inscriptions, few of which are now visible. In the church-yard is a monument to the memory of Alderman William Jones and his wife, the former of whom died in 1612. It formerly stood in the chantry north of the chancel; and about sixteen years ago it was munificently repaired by the late Sir Thomas Tyrwhit Jones, Bart, M.P. the worthy and respected representative of the family.

The living is in the gift of the crown. Its present incumbent the Rev. J. Wightman.

St. Giles's Church,

Of the origin of which no authentic account is known, stands at the eastern extremity of the Abbey Foregate, and bears marks of considerable antiquity. By some it has been thought to be the earliest parochial foundation in Shrewsbury; but others, with more semblance of truth, give the palm in this respect to the Abbey, to which St. Giles's is now attached, merely as a convenience for the performance of funeral ceremonies; public worship being only celebrated within its walls, twice every year.

It is a small plain building, consisting of a nave, chancel, and north aisle, with a small turret for the reception of a bell. Its interior presents several varieties of architecture, whilst its antique and worm-eaten benches, its homely pavement, and its almost altogether unadorned state, combine to give it a simply interesting appearance.

The church-yard contains the tombs of various inhabitants of the town; among others is one raised to the memory of Cheney Hart, M.D. a native of Warrington, and an eminent physician of this town for thirty-three years, on the pedestal of which, crowned with a handsome urn is a Latin inscription. On the north side the yard is a tomb in memory of William Congreve, esq. formerly lieutenant-colonel of the 17th foot, and his relict Jane. This gentleman was a descendant of the ancient family which gave birth to our celebrated dramatic writer, while his lady, a Waller, was sprung from that of elegant poet of Beaconsfield. The grave stone of William White, who was a quarter-master of horse in the reign of William III. bears the following lines:

In Irish wars I fought for England's glory;
Let no man scoff at telling of the story:
I saw great Schomberg fall, likewise the brave St. Ruth,
And here I come to die, not there in my youth.
Thro' dangers great I've passed many a storm;
Die we must all as sure as we are born.

PROTESTANT DISSENTERS.

IT is always painful to men of sober and moderate principles, to recur to the Act of Uniformity, which in Bartholomew's day, 1662, drove from their livings at least 2000 clergymen, "many of them distinguished by their abilities and zeal," to seek subsistence from the charity of friends, and consolation in times of oppression from the calm testimony of a good conscience. To this act however, Shrewsbury is indebted for its first regular dissenting church. The place where they assembled is called

The Presbyterian Chapel.

This congregation was founded by Mr. Bryan and Mr. Tallents, the ministers ejected from St. Chad's and St. Mary's. It was destroyed in 1715, by a mob, soon after the accession of the House of Hanover, and was rebuilt by government. It stands on the north side of the High Street, and is a plain building of brick, neatly fitted up. It is now used by a respectable congregation of Unitarian Dissenters. Minister, the Rev. G. Case.

In the year 1766, a disagreement took place among the congregation frequenting the Presbyterian chapel, relative to the choice of a minister, in consequence of which, they separated, and a part of them erected a new chapel. It is called

The Independent Chapel,

Situate on Swan Hill, and is a commodious brick erection of an oblong form. It has a numerous and very respectable society. On the north side is a vestry. A neat stone tablet on the front bears the following inscription:

> THIS BUILDING WAS ERECTED
> IN THE YEAR 1767,
> FOR THE PUBLIC WORSHIP OF GOD
> AND IN DEFENCE OF THE
> RIGHTS OF MAJORITIES
> IN PROTESTANT DISSENTING
> CONGREGATIONS
> TO CHOOSE THEIR OWN MINISTERS.

Minister, the Rev. T. Weaver.

The Methodist Chapel,

Called also St. John's Chapel, is situate on St. John's Hill, and previous to the erection of a house in front of part of it, was a great ornament to the street. It is a neat and extensive brick building of an oblong form, and is calculated to accommodate a large congregation. Behind the chapel is a vestry, in which are placed the stairs leading to the pulpit, which in consequence, has rather a novel appearance to a stranger, no steps being visible in the chapel. The congregation is numerous and respectable.

The Baptist Chapel

Is in Dog Lane; with a well-finished interior, it is, perhaps, from the awkward situation of the pulpit and its extreme lowness, one of the most unpleasant chapels in the town, especially when crowded, which is often the case on particular occasions. It is a plain respectable brick building, and has a numerous congregation. The Baptists were established here in 1780.

The Quaker's or Friends Meeting House

Is situate on St. John's Hill, and, like the respectable body who assemble within its walls, is a plain unadorned building.

The SANDEMANIANS and WELSH METHODISTS, also have Chapels in Hill's Lane; and the ROMAN CATHOLICS a neat one near the Town Walls at the back of the Lion Inn.

CHARITABLE ERECTIONS & INSTITUTIONS.

The Free Schools.

EDUCATION is, in the British empire, an object of national concern. Our various universities and public schools are splendid monuments of the attention paid by our ancestors to the important object of training and enlightening the youthful mind. The provision made for the support of these establishments, especially in England and Ireland, is, generally speaking, munificent. At the same time, it is not sufficient to afford a temptation to the indulgence of idleness, by the conversion of respectable offices into sinecures. The dignity hence accruing to their teachers and professors, invests them with high authority, and imparts additional weight to their instructions; while the respect in which they are habitually held by long established prescription, gives a powerful sanction to the system of their discipline.

This observation applies with peculiar force to the munificent edifice of the Royal Free School of King Edward VI. which is situate at the northern extremity of Castle Street. Its erection was completed in 1630, the ancient school-room, which was composed of timber, having been removed in order to the completion of the present spacious and convenient structure of free-stone. The building surrounds two sides of the court with a square pinnacled tower in the angle. In the centre of the front is a gateway, adorned on each side with a Corinthian column, very rudely designed, upon which stand the statues of a scholar and a graduate, bareheaded, and in the dress of the times. Over the arch is a Greek sentence from Isocrates,

> Ἐὰν ᾖς φιλομαθὴς ἔσῃ πολυμαθής.

Importing that a love of literature is necessary to the formation of a scholar. Above are the arms of Charles I. The ground floor on one side the gateway, contains a room originally used as an accidence school; on the other the third master's house, now given to the head master, who places his assistant in it. In the middle story are comprised the lodging rooms of the assistant's house, and the lower master's apartment, which for many years has been converted into a writing school. The principal school room, which occupies the upper story, is 80 feet by 21.

The chapel is on the ground floor of the other part of the building, and is divided from the anti-chapel by a handsome open screen of oak, richly embellished with grotesque carving, as are the pulpit and bible stand. The ceiling is adorned with a variety of foliage, devices, and rebusses, preserved from the ruins of St. Alkmond's Church. The arms of the first and present masters are placed along the middle. Prayers are read here twice on school days, by the head master, who is chaplain and catechist, for which he has a distinct salary of £20 a year.

Over the chapel, and of the same size, is the library, which contains a most valuable collection of books, and in size and decoration is in no respect inferior to the majority of those in the Universities. A half length of Henry VIII. and his son Edward VI. when a boy; a full length of an Admiral in the dress of Charles II. reign, probably Benbow, together with five portraits of head masters, ornament the walls. In this room are also preserved three sepulchral stones discovered at Wroxeter.

A small museum is separated from the lower end of the room, in which are some Roman antiquities, chiefly from Wroxeter, with a few fossils and other natural curiosities. Among the latter, is the dried body of a sturgeon, caught in 1802, in a weir adjoining the island, a quarter of a mile below the castle. When alive, it weighed 192 pounds, and was 9 feet long and 3 feet 4 inches round.

In front of the schools on the town side, is a play ground enclosed from the street by iron railing, and a considerable piece of ground is used for a similar purpose at the back, which opens to the country and is entirely secluded from the town. Two large houses most delightfully situated contiguous, belong to the masters, with every accommodation for boarders. The revenues are very handsome, and are derived chiefly from the tithes of a number of townships in the parishes of St. Mary and St. Chad, and the whole rectory of Chirbury, which were granted by King Edward VI. and Queen Elizabeth.

This seminary has been long celebrated for the erudition of its scholars. Under the "excellent and worthie" Thomas Ashton, it flourished eminently. At one period he had 290 pupils, among whom we notice Sir Henry Sydney, whose son, the heroic Sir Philip Sydney, laid here the seeds of that exemplary friendship with the celebrated Sir Fulk Greville, Lord Brook, which he maintained through the whole of his short but splendid career. Beside these, the noted Jeffries, Lord Chief Justices Jones and Price; Drs. Bowers and Thomas, Bishops of Chichester and Salisbury; the Rev. John Taylor, L.L.D. and the celebrated Dr. Waring, received their education here. Nor does the present character of the school fall short of that distinguished pre-eminence which it formerly sustained. Under the judicious direction of the learned Dr. Butler, it is in a flourishing state. Not only do the children of the principal families in the adjacent counties and North Wales, receive the rudiments of their learning here, but also those of many families of distinction from distant parts of the empire. The appointment of master rests solely in the fellows of St. John's College, Cambridge; that of ushers and the mode of instruction is vested in the head master.

The House of Industry.

This handsome brick building, situated on the opposite side of the river to the Quarry, was erected in 1765, as a Foundling Hospital, at an expence of £12,000. Numbers of children were sent here from London, and placed out at nurse during their infancy with the neighbouring cottagers, under the superintendance of the surrounding gentry. When arrived at a proper age, they were brought into this house and employed in various branches of a woollen manufactory, and afterwards apprenticed to various individuals. About 1774, however, the governors finding their funds inadequate to the support of the charity, the house was shut up; and a few years after was rented by government, who in the American war used it as a place of confinement for Dutch prisoners.

In 1784, an act of parliament was obtained to incorporate the five parishes of Shrewsbury and Meole Brace, as far as related to their poor, and to erect a general House of Industry. The governors of the Foundling Charity were glad of an opportunity to dispose of their erection at a considerably reduced rate, and the building was accordingly purchased, together with about twenty acres of land, for about £5,500, and it was opened for the reception of paupers in December in that year. For a short period they were employed in the fabrication of woollen cloths, but this being found injurious to the pecuniary resources of the house, it was discontinued, and at present their employment chiefly consists in manufacturing the various articles of their clothing. They breakfast, dine, and sup in the dining hall, a very long room, the men, women, boys and girls, being each placed at separate tables. Divine service is performed twice each Sunday, in a neat chapel parallel with the hall. There is also an infirmary, where the sick and infirm are lodged in proper wards, and attended to by nurses and the apothecary belonging to the house. The whole is under the management of twelve directors, chosen from persons assessed in the associated parishes at £15. or possessed of property to the amount of £30. per ann. who appoint a governor and matron, to superintend the domestic economy of the establishment.

Mr. Nield, the worthy disciple of the philanthropic Howard, remarks of this place, which he visited in 1807, "This House of Industry is certainly a house of plenty, for the books every where, bear record of good living, and the famous beef slaughtered here. The average number in the house is 340; the children delicate and pampered, from being accustomed to abundance and variety of provisions, and comfortable rooms, very dissimilar to the hardy peasant, and therefore ill calculated to rear up useful assistances in the employments of agriculture, or to make useful servants in this agricultural county. They would prefer a race of hardy lads, inured from their infancy to combat weather and temporary want; whose nerves are strong by early exertions, and their understandings furnished with some knowledge of rural life."—Mr. Nield's extensive observation and experience, qualified him to judge of the most proper aliment and employment of this class of persons, far better than most of the directors and governors of similar institutions can reasonably be expected to do; and as indulgence and plenty cannot be supposed to be the portion of the children of the poor in their progress through life, we may indulge a hope that the directors will speedily devise some plan for the initiation of their young dependants into habits of judicious labour and healthy abstinence.

Along the north front of the house is a beautiful gravel walk, from whence the town is seen to great advantage. On the right, the Abbey-foregate, with its two venerable churches, various manufactories, Lord Hill's Column, and a great extent of fertile land, are seen backed by the Wrekin, Haughmond Hill, &c. In front, the river Severn flowing close underneath, the beautiful verdure of the quarry, and the town, present themselves; whilst on the left are descried a large portion of this extremely fertile county, together with the distant Montgomeryshire and Denbighshire hills. This extensive prospect over the neighbouring country, with the endless variety of scenes that present themselves to the spectator are finely described in the following lines:

> Ever charming, ever new,
> When will the landscape tire the view?
> The fountain's fall, the river's flow,
> The wooded vallies warm and low;
> The windy summits wild and high
> Roughly rushing on the sky!
> The pleasing seat, the ruin'd tow'r,
> The naked rock, the shady bow'r
> The town and village dome and farm
> Each give each a double charm,
> As pearls upon an Ethiop's arm.
>
> DYER.

It was from this house, that the benevolent but eccentric Mr. Day, deluded by the fascinating eloquence Rosseau, selected two girls on whom to try an experiment on female education, in which he proposed to unite the delicacy of a modern female, with the bold simplicity of a Spartan virgin, which should despise the frivolity and dissipation of the present corrupted age.

Having obtained the object of his wishes, he repaired with them to France, taking no English servant, in order that they might receive no ideas but those which he chose to instil. After spending about eight months in France, he placed the one in a respectable situation in London, and with his favourite actually proceeded some years in the execution of his project; but experience and mature reflection at length convinced him, that his theory of education was impractible, and he renounced all hope of moulding his protegee after the model his fancy had formed. He therefore placed her in a boarding school at Sutton Coldfield, in Warwickshire; and after completing her education, she resided some years in Birmingham, and subsequently at Newport, in this county: and by her amiable deportment secured a large circle of friends. Mr. Day frequently corresponded with her parentally. In her 26th year she married Mr. Bicknell, a gentleman who accompanied Mr. D. to Shrewsbury, at the commencement of this singular experiment.

Salop Infirmary.

This noble asylum, situated in St. Mary's Churchyard, was formed in the memorable year 1745, for the accommodation and relief of the diseased and indigent poor. The munificence with which this excellent institution has been supported by the inhabitants of the county at large, has enabled its conductors to proceed upon the most liberal principles. Admission is given to the diseased from whatever quarter they may come, provided they are recommended by a subscriber; but in case of sudden accident, this recommendation is dispensed with.

It was opened in 1747, and has the honour of being one of the earliest of similar erections, those of Bristol, Northampton, Winchester, and Exeter, being the only provincial ones established prior thereto. The building is of brick with a stone portal, and the back windows, which look into the country, command a varied and extensive prospect. Considered with respect to its internal cleanliness and economical management, and the humane and skilful attentions of the medical gentlemen of the town, its advantages are such as will vie with those of any similar provincial institution, and are calculated to excite in the minds of the benevolent and reflecting, feelings of the most compassionate regard and generous sensibility.

Since its foundation, £126,671. 9s. 10d. in voluntary subscriptions and benefactions, has been contributed for its maintenance and support. By the last report it appears, that up to June 1822, 33,589 in-patients have been received into the house, 18,373 have been cured, and 3,481 relieved; also 52,142 out-patients, of whom 37,720 have been cured, and 4,877 relieved.

Besides the physicians and surgeons of the town who attend gratuitously, a surgeon resides in the house, in order that medical aid may not be wanting in cases of emergency. The domestic economy is superintended by a matron. The pecuniary concerns are managed by a secretary, under the inspection of a Board of Directors and deputy Treasurer. A Treasurer also is appointed annually from among the subscribers of five guineas and upwards, and on the Friday in the Shrewsbury race week, a sermon is preached by the chaplain, and a collection made for the benefit of the charity, the plates being held by two ladies, supported by two gentlemen of distinguished rank or opulence. The clergy of the established church, residing in the town, officiate in rotation weekly; two of the subscribers also resident in Shrewsbury, are weekly appointed as house visitors.

Millington's Hospital

Stands in the suburb of Frankwell, and is so called from its benevolent founder, the late Mr. James Millington, draper of Shrewsbury, who in 1734, bequeathed nearly the whole of his property to its erection.

The hospital is a respectable building of brick. Over the pediment, in the centre, is a turret, in which is a clock. In this part is a chapel, used also for a school room, and houses for the master and mistress. On each side are six small houses for the poor.

The will of Mr. Millington appointed a schoolmaster and mistress, who have each a house and £40. per annum, and the master £10. additional for keeping the accounts. A chaplain, with a stipend of £25. Twelve poor men or women chosen from the single housekeepers of Frankwell, or the part of St. Chad's parish nearest to it, to each of whom is allotted an apartment in the hospital, consisting of two comfortable rooms, a small garden, a gown or coat, given on St. Thomas's day, a load of coals on All Saints' day, and an allowance of £6. per annum. Gowns or coats and 40*s.* each, are also dispensed every year to ten poor single housekeepers resident in Frankwell, and when a vacancy happens in the hospital, the person who has longest received the garments is elected to it. The hospitallers and out-pensioners have also two twopenny loaves weekly. Twenty poor boys and as many poor girls, born in Frankwell, are completely clothed twice annually, and receive their education in the hospital. When arrived at the age of fourteen, the boys are apprenticed, £7. 10*s.* is given with each, and £2. 10*s.* is expended in cloathing: £5. is also presented to those, who at the expiration of their first year's apprenticeship, can bring a certificate of their good behaviour. The girls are allowed £5. on going out apprentices.

Two exhibitions of £40. a year each are founded for students of St. Magdalen's College, Cambridge. Those who have been originally scholars on the hospital foundation, claim the preference, or one born in Frankwell, and educated in the free grammar school is most eligible.

Allatt's School

Was erected in 1800, at the bottom of Swan Hill, pursuant to the will of the late Mr. John Allatt, formerly chamberlain to the corporation of Shrewsbury.

The structure is of free-stone, and contains two houses for the master and mistress, connected with the school rooms by arcades. It cost about £2000, erected from a plan by Mr. Haycock. The interest of the residue of Mr. Allatt's property, maintains a schoolmaster and mistress, and educates twenty poor boys, and as many girls, whose parents have not received parochial relief. The children are taught reading, writing, and arithmetic, and the girls sewing; they are cloathed once a year, and at a proper age apprenticed. Twenty coats and eighty good stuff gowns are also distributed annually, to that number of poor old men and women.

Bowler's School,

In the Back Lane, near the Wyle Cop, is a plain brick building, founded in 1724, pursuant to the will of Mr. Thomas Bowdler, alderman and draper, for instructing, cloathing, and apprenticing poor children, of the parish of St. Julian. The dress is blue.

Public Subscription Charity School

Was erected near the Abbey church, in 1778. The institution is supported by voluntary subscription, and children from every part of the town, boys as well as girls are admissible. The system of instruction pursued is that of Dr. Bell, the master having a salary of £40. and the mistress £30. The dress of the children is brown, and hence it is sometimes called the brown school. The number in the school at the date of the last report, June 1822, were, boys 190—girls 150.

Royal Lancasterian School.

This edifice was built in 1812, in consequence of a lecture delivered on the subject of Education, by the celebrated Joseph Lancaster, at the Town Hall, in Shrewsbury. As its name imports, the system of instruction is that of Mr. Lancaster. There is one apartment for boys and one for girls, to each of which children are admitted, on being recommended by subscribers. It is supported by voluntary subscriptions and donations. Number of boys 260; girls 217.

St. Chad's Alms-Houses.

> "This yeare 1409, one Bennett Tupton, being a common Beere Bruar, and dwellinge in St. Chadd's Churche Yarde in Shrousberie, now called the Colledge, founded the Almeshouses in the sayde St. Chadd's Churche Yarde in Shrousberie, beinge then a man at that tyme of 60 yeares of age."

Originally they were 13 in number, but not having any funds, two are fallen to decay. The present allowance to the poor is about 16s. per annum, including 2s. 2d. paid by the company of mercers.

St. Mary's Alms-Houses,

Situate at the western end of St. Mary's church-yard, were founded 1460, by Degory Watur, draper. They are 16 in number, extremely wretched and filthy in appearance, and dangerous and unwholesome from their smallness, each having only a single apartment 11 feet by 8, without any outlet. The centre house, originally inhabited by the founder, and called the hall, is larger than the others, and has a wooden porch, on which is a painting of Watur and his wife, and on the front is the effigy of King Edward IV. The poor people, who must be parishioners of St. Mary's, have each £2. 6s. 10½d. allowed them annually, by quarterly payments from the draper's company, and an upper garment once in two years.

St. Giles' Alms-Houses,

Near St. Giles' church, in the Abbey Foregate. The houses are four in number. The residents in them are nominated by the earl of Tankerville, who allows them 1*s.* 6*d.* per week, with a quantity of coals and an upper garment annually.

Sick Man's Friend and Lying-In Charity.

The objects of this Institution, which was begun in 1810, are the relief of the diseased, and of poor married women in childbed, at their own houses; who not only receive medical assistance, if necessary, but the use of bed linen, food and every other necessary that their situation requires. The meetings of the Committee are held at the Independent Chapel, on Swanhill.

Samaritan Society & Lying-In Charity,

Is similar in its objects and institution to the former. Its operations commenced in 1814, and the meetings of its Committee are held in the vestry of St. John's Chapel.

Ladies' Charity,

Was instituted in 1814, by some benevolent females, solely for the purpose of assisting poor married women with cloathing, food, and other necessaries requisite for their situation. The meetings of the Committee are held in the vestry of St. Chad's church.

The extensive scale on which the three last named charities are conducted, and the liberality with which their benefits are dispensed, to the deserving poor, place them among the first charitable institutions which so much distinguish the town of Shrewsbury. Their operations are confined to no sect or party, and they design nothing but the purest philanthropy. Their laudable plans are promoted by the individual exertions and charitable subscriptions of the members, each of whom pay 2*s.* per quarter and upwards. The number of the members is about 300. No public buildings are connected with these praise-worthy establishments, the present mode of relief being considered superior to those of an hospital.

Shrewsbury General Sunday School

Is held in the large room in the linen manufactory in Coleham. The order and regularity observed in this institution has been noticed by strangers from distant parts of the kingdom. Its numbers according to the last report were boys 215, girls 247. In addition to this, a separate room is allotted to the instruction of Adult scholars, whose number is 44. The whole are taught reading and writing.

Swan Hill Sunday School

Is a similar institution and similarly conducted. The number of scholars are, boys 96, girls 104.

Besides this, St. Chad's Boys Sunday School, has about 100 boys, under the superintendance of its committee.

St. Mary's Sunday and Day School

Is held in the chapel of St. Mary's church. The children are taught reading and writing; their number is about 162.

St. Chad's Ladies' School.

This is carried on in that part of St. Chad's old church which escaped entire destruction. It is a most praise-worthy establishment, and is superintended by many respectable ladies of St. Chad's parish, who devote a considerable portion of their time in furtherance of this object of their anxious solicitude.

The latter institutions deserve the close inspection of the benevolent and humane. The recurrence of stated days, on which the well-ordered artizan and peasant, emerging from the dirt and impurities of their vocations, to practice the virtue of cleanliness, produces an easy association between a sense of self-decency, and the reverence due to the service for which the sabbath is set apart. To strengthen this feeling and principle, becomes therefore an important object to all those interested in the good order, peace and happiness of the people of the British empire; and to enfix it as deeply as possible, the impression cannot be made too early.

Society for Promoting Christian Knowledge.

In conjunction with this excellent institution, a District Society has been established here for the purpose of co-operating with the Society at Bartlett's Buildings, in the distribution of Bibles, Testaments, Prayer Books, and other religious books and tracts. The praise-worthy objects of the Society are supported by some of the most respectable and opulent residents in the county.—Secretary, the Rev. Archdeacon Owen, M.A., F.A.S.

Shropshire Bible Society

An auxiliary Bible Society, to co-operate with the British and Foreign Bible Society, in London, was instituted here on the 11th of November, 1811. The late Rev. Francis Leighton, explained to the meeting, summoned on this occasion, the nature and objects of this charity. A number of liberal donations were offered, and an extensive annual subscription entered into. The important object of this society, as its name imports, is, the gratuitous distribution of the scriptures among the poor inhabitants, and also by its contributions, to aid the noble design of the parent society in translating the Bible into all languages which are represented by letters, and to circulate them throughout the earth. The Rev. Archdeacon Corbett is the president, and the annual meeting is held on the first Wednesday in July.

REMAINS OF ANCIENT BUILDINGS.

The Council House

Received its name from having been the residence of the Court of the Marches of Wales; for though their principal abode was at Ludlow, they were accustomed to hold one term in the year at this place, for the convenience of suitors, and another at Bewdley, and sometimes at Hereford.

The house is in the immediate vicinity of the castle (in the outer court of which, it is supposed to have been built,) on a steep bank overhanging the river. The entrance to it from the town is by a venerable timber gate-house, the ornaments of which have lately been plastered over. The great hall and chamber, which were the only apartments not *modernized*, have just (1815) been pulled down and rebuilt, and the rich old chimney-piece which stood in the hall, in the centre of which were the arms of Owen of Condover, has been removed to that venerable mansion. Charles I. kept his court here, as also did James II. in 1687.

St. Nicholas's Chapel

Is still standing in part on the left hand entrance to the council house, and is now used as a stable. The building consisted of a nave and chancel without aisle; the former is nearly perfect, and there is no doubt, but that its erection is of great antiquity. The whole length is 50 feet, the breadth 19 feet.

Austin's Friars.

The convent of the Eremites of St. Augustine, stood at the bottom of Barker-Street [89], near the river. A small part only remains, little of it being to be seen excepting the shell of a large building of red stone, with two pointed arched door ways. It is now used as a tan-house.

Franciscan Friary.

The house of the Franciscan or Grey Friars, stood under the Wyle Cop, on the banks of the Severn. A part of this friary still remains, converted into houses. A large stone coffin lies in the garden of an old timber house, erected soon after the dissolution.

Dominican Friary.

Scarcely a fragment of this friary now remains. It is supposed to have occupied nearly the whole of the meadow between the Water-lane-gate and the English Bridge.

The lady of king Edward IV. twice lay in at this convent, and was delivered of Richard and George Plantagenet. The former perished in the tower with his unfortunate elder brother, in the subsequent reign, by the machinations of his cruel uncle Richard. Prince George died young.

PLACES OF AMUSEMENT.

The Theatre.

THIS building, if we may credit the affirmation of Phillips, is part of the ancient palace of the princes of Powisland; who in their frequent transactions with the sovereigns of England, often resided at Shrewsbury. John de Charlton, who married an heiress of the line of Powis, obtained a license in 1308, to embattle this mansion, and hence it acquired the name of Charlton Hall. In 1445, Henry Gray, Earl of Tankerville and of Powis, granted the premises to Thomas Bromley; from whom, twenty-five years after, they were demised to Nycholas Warynge, of Salop, merchant of the staple of Calais. After various changes and transfers, it became the property of the Waring family.

The ancient boundary walls of this mansion, inclosed all the space contained between Cross Hill, St. John's Hill, Murivance, or Swan Hill, and Shoplache. The house doubtless formed one, if not two quadrangles, which may still be traced. The most considerable remnant is a building of red stone, in length 100 feet, and in breadth 31 feet, which is the present Theatre. The side next the street has been plastered and washed with stone colour, to give it the semblance of a modern front; but surely, nothing was ever so disgraceful to the town as its present appearance, especially when considered as a public building. The other side exhibits the original walls with some blocked-up pointed arches, and other features of high antiquity. It is probable, that in the old edifice, this part was the great chamber, appointed according to the usage of the times, for receiving company, and occasionally for exhibiting shows and interludes. The interior being now fitted up as a modern Theatre, retains few of its original appurtenances, except the remains of a small spiral stone staircase. It consists of a pretty roomy pit, a ground tier of boxes, with upper side boxes, and a tolerably spacious gallery. The stage is well adapted to the size of the place, and the decorations are in the usual style of provincial playhouses. The same remark may apply to the performers, who are, generally of that middling class, which consists of persons in their first career to excellence, and of others that have got half-way, and remain stationary. The taste of the Salopians being rather of the retired kind, which delights most in domestic society, does not contribute much to encourage dramatic exhibitions, and the house is scarcely ever crowded, except during the race week, and in the summer visits of the London performers. The audiences, however, if not numerous, are select; and it may be mentioned to their honour, that they never tolerate any thing that borders on buffoonery and indecorum. One of their most favourite plays, for obvious reasons, is the first part of Henry IV. and when Jack Falstaff talks of having fought Hotspur "a full hour by Shrewsbury clock," he never fails to draw down a thunder of applause.

Assembly Room.

An elegant apartment erected for this polite amusement, at the back of the Lion inn, and is extremely commodious, having a gallery for the musicians at the northern end. The dancing and card assemblies commence in the month of September, and are held generally once a month. The town and neighbourhood of Shrewsbury furnishing a variety of genteel society, they are generally attended by a very numerous and respectable company. They are supported by subscription.

The Circus

Is a spacious brick erection, near the Welsh Bridge. It was built in 1821 by Mr. Newton, and as its name imports, is used principally as a Theatre for the display of Equestrian performances. It is spacious and commodious, and well calculated for Pantomimical exhibitions.

Races.

The Horse Races continue for three days, and take place in the month of September. On these days a great number of plates, sweepstakes and matches are run for; the course is at Bicton Heath, about two miles west of the town, where booths are erected for the use of spectators. The gentlemen who are annually appointed stewards, generally being persons of property and influence, the races are well attended, not only by the population of the neighbourhood, but also by many families of the first respectability from distant parts of the kingdom.

Fishing.

The Severn is celebrated for the excellency of its salmon, which was formerly in such abundance at Shrewsbury, that it was made an article in the indentures of apprentices, that they were not to be obliged to eat it oftener than two days in a week. Of its superabundance the inhabitants cannot at least now complain, little being to be purchased under 2s. 6d. per pound, and that but seldom.

Besides Salmon, the river Severn contains twenty-one other sorts of fish, the chief of which are flounders, pike, trout, perch, eels, shad, carp, lamperns, and lampreys. The two latter are found in many other rivers, but none are so much valued as those taken out of the Severn, from whence they are sent to many parts of England. Lampreys are a delicious dish, but unwholesome if eaten in great quantities: of which we have an instance in the death of Henry I. who died in consequence of eating too plentifully of this fish.

Nor is it in the Severn alone that the angler will find amusement, Meole and Condover brooks affording excellent trout, and the river Tern, a great variety of delicate fish. Each of these streams are within a short distance of the town.

Bowling Greens.

Of this most healthful species of amusement Shrewsbury cannot boast; however, the pleasant villages of Meole, distant one mile, and Uffington, distant three miles and a half, furnish two very excellent greens, and where the pedestrian will be well accommodated and attended to, after the fatigues of his walk.

PUBLIC ACCOMMODATIONS.

Water.

WITH this most necessary article Shrewsbury is abundantly supplied, and it is also of a most excellent quality. The first we shall notice, is that which is chiefly used for drinking, and is obtained from the

Conduits,

which are placed in several situations about the town for the general convenience of the inhabitants. The spring which supplies these fountains, rises at *Broadwell*, in a field near Crow-Meole, about two miles from the town. The work of conducting it to town in leaden pipes, was completed about 1574; a reservoir was placed under a shop in the Butcher Row in 1743, but was afterwards removed to Claremont Hill, and on the demolition of the town-walls, for the purpose of erecting the new church of St. Chad on its site, the lodge opposite the Quarry-keeper's house, at the top of the centre walk of that beautiful promenade, was built for this purpose.

Severn Water.

The reservoir for this water is in a large cistern near the butter market, from whence it is conveyed to almost all the inhabitants by means of lead pipes, for which they pay in proportion to the quantity of water. The water is forced up to this reservoir by means of a large wheel placed at the English or East Bridge, but in consequence of the frequent fluctuations of the Severn, it is probable that six months out of the twelve, the town is destitute of this supply, and whatever quantity may be wanted for culinary and other purposes is carried from the river. It is much to be wished, that the present waterworks were removed, not only on account of the deformity which they give to the noble appearance of the bridge; but the water which is sent to the reservoir after running nearly round the town and receiving all its filth, would by the removal of the works to Cotton Hill, and the erection of a steam engine, be distributed to the inhabitants in a more regular manner, and in a much purer state.

Baths.

There are two cold baths, one in Kingsland and the other in the suburb of Abbey Foregate, but neither of them can be recommended as possessing suitable accommodations, especially when compared with those of other places.

The Quarry.

This beautiful walk is on the western side of the town near the church of St. Chad; it occupies a rich meadow of about twenty acres gradually sloping to the river, and is supposed to have obtained its name from a small quarry of soft red sand-stone, which was formerly procured here, and with which some of the ancient buildings were no doubt erected. The lower walk which skirts the river, is 540 yards in length, shaded with lime trees, planted by Henry Jenks, Esq. in the year of his mayoralty, 1719. Three walks lead from the town to that on the bank of the Severn, and two others formerly crossed the entrance.

Few promenades in the kingdom can vie with the Quarry, particularly in the spring of the year, when it displays all its pride of beauty. Its spacious fields carpeted with grass, thickly studded with the golden hue of the butter cup, and the silvery tinge of the modest daisy—its noble trees clothed with leafy verdure of various hues, and protecting the pedestrian from the piercing rays of the sun—the Severn rolling its broad and majestic stream along—whilst the feathered songsters carol their notes to the God of nature, altogether present a lovely picture of rural happiness. Nor is the Quarry at "the fall of the leaf" when nature unburdens herself of her lovely mantle, unworthy the contemplation of the reflecting mind.

> The fading foliage of th' embrowning grove,
> (Which oft has listened to the voice of love,)
> In mournful junction with the shortning day,
> Reminds us of the circling year's decay:
> While the fleet, whistling winds, dismantling, tear
> Each tree's green honours to the chilling air,
> Thence to descend, and in man's footsteps lie
> A just memento of mortality.

In the 16th century, it appears that Shrewsbury was the scene of theatrical representations. Julian the apostate, was performed here in 1565, and two years afterwards, the Passion of Christ, to see which queen Elizabeth is said to have come as far as Coventry, but on learning that its representation was over, returned to London. The particular spot which formed the rural theatre, was at the top of the rope walk in the Quarry. The ground which forms a gentle acclivity, was cut into the form of an amphitheatre, the seats of which may still be traced in the bank.

Beside this, which is the chief walk, the town and neighbourhood furnish such a variety of picturesque and pleasing promenades as are equalled perhaps by few in the kingdom.

MANUFACTORIES.

ALTHOUGH Shrewsbury is not distinguished by its spirit of commercial enterprise, its contiguity to the Principality, the facilities which it possesses for the importation and exportation of goods, by means of its noble river and canals, and its situation as the capital of an extensive and populous county, combine to give to it many advantages over a variety of places equally insular. Its fabrication of threads, linen cloths, &c. &c. stand unrivalled; whilst the more common articles of domestic life are executed in a stile of neatness, certainly equal, if not superior, to those of any other place of similar size. The following are the principal, which we can do little more than enumerate.

Messrs. BENYONS' MANUFACTORY is built on the north bank of the Severn, near the prison. The articles manufactured here consist of linen yarns, cloths, canvas, and threads. The building was erected in 1804. The process of making the various articles, is carried on by upwards of 400 hands, and the whole machinery, which is of wonderful construction, is worked by the solemn and stupendous action of a steam engine of 55 horse power, which keeps in continual motion upwards of 3000 spindles.

A short distance from the former stands the FACTORY of Messrs. MARSHALL and Co. who manufacture similar articles, the whole of whose machinery is also worked by the powerful agency of steam.

Of a like description is that also of Mr. BAGE, in Coleham. The other establishments are HAZLEDINE's, and GITTINS and CARTWRIGHT's IRON FOUNDRIES, the BREWERY of JOHN HEATHCOTE and Co.—the FLANNEL FACTORIES of Mr. BAKER and Mr. RAMSBOTHAM—and Mr. HILL's SPIRIT DISTILLERY.

Nor will it be improper under this head, to mention some others, which, although not strictly speaking, manufactures, do honour to the town, and are worthy the early attention of strangers. Among the first of these, may be named BROCAS's CHINA and GLASS REPOSITORY, in the Castle-street. The splendid collection here exhibited of antique and foreign china, together with the no less beautiful and admired specimens of the same article, from the first manufactories of this kingdom, and the rich and superb display of glass in an endless variety of patterns, as well for use as ornament, cannot fail to prove a rich treat to the stranger.

BETTON and EVANS's STAINED GLASS MANUFACTORY, where great improvements have been made in that beautiful art. The perfection at which they have arrived, is truly astonishing, and they have the merit of approaching nearest (and in some colours even surpassing) the brilliant tints of the ancients. That this eulogium is not undeserved, may be ascertained by viewing the splendid windows executed by them for

Lichfield cathedral, as well as the specimens which may be inspected at their warehouse on Wyle Cop.

The MARBLE ROOMS of Mr. CARLINE, sculptor, modeller, and marble mason, Abbey Foregate; where a variety of marble chimney-pieces are exhibited, in the Egyptian, Grecian, Gothic, and modern tastes, and in various species of the most beautiful foreign and British marbles. Marble tables for halls, sideboards, &c. various figures in marble, bronze, artificial stone, to support dials and lamps; statues, busts, &c. of excellent execution.

MARKETS.

THE markets of Shrewsbury are plentifully supplied with the luxuries and conveniences of life. They are held on Wednesdays and Saturdays. The first is small; that on Saturday is, perhaps, not surpassed in the display of eatables, by the market of any town of a similar size in the kingdom. Butcher's meat is sold at the single and double rows on Pride Hill, and at the Shambles in Fish-street. Butter, Eggs, and Poultry of every description at the Butter Market. The green market is held in the square before the town-hall, where there is generally a luxuriant supply of vegetables, and of extremely early production. Wheat and all sorts of grain are disposed of in the market-house. With milk the inhabitants are tolerably well supplied by persons of the town who keep cows expressly for the purpose; but "art, ever jealous of nature, and benevolently careful of the stomachs of the inhabitants, has, by the application of a certain useful element, wisely deprived it of its luxuriant richness."

The Fish market is well supplied. Not only the Severn salmon, which is caught at their doors, but a very considerable quantity of different descriptions of the finny tribe from Wales, are regularly exposed for sale at tolerably moderate prices. For its excellent brawn, Shrewsbury has long been distinguished.

Fairs.

Fairs are held here on the second Tuesday and Wednesday in every month.

MISCELLANEOUS NOTICES AND REFERENCES.

Inns and Taverns.

THE LION INN, on Wyle Cop, is kept by Mr. Tompkins. For elegant accommodation and the greatest attention, it is not surpassed. The London, Holyhead, Newtown, and Ludlow mails run to this house; also coaches regularly from hence to London, Holyhead, Worcester, Hereford, Bath, Cheltenham, Birmingham, Chester, Liverpool, Manchester, and all parts of the kingdom.

THE TALBOT INN, in Shoplatch, is kept by Mr. Jobson. Extensive premises with requisite accommodations. Coaches run from this house similarly to those from the Lion.

THE RAVEN INN, in Castle-street. A spacious and convenient house, with excellent accommodation. As a house frequented by commercial gentlemen, it ranks first in the town.

THE RAVEN AND BELL INN, on the Wyle Cop, has extensive and good accommodations for travellers, and is well frequented.

THE CROWN INN, near the Butter Cross, is centrically situated, and travellers meet with civility and attention.

Besides these, there are numerous others, which cannot here be detailed, but in all of them of respectable name, the stranger will experience a civility and attention which in houses of this description are not in all places to be met with.

Public Offices.

THE POST OFFICE is kept in Dogpole. It opens at seven in the morning and closes at nine at night, and is shut during divine service on Sundays. To London the mail goes out daily at eleven o'clock (except Saturday.) To Holyhead and Ireland every evening at three o'clock. To Ludlow, Hereford, and South Wales every morning at eleven. To Chester, through Ellesmere and Wrexham every evening at three o'clock. To Pool, and all Merionethshire, (except Bala and Corwen) Aberystwith, every evening about half past three o'clock, and to Whitchurch, Wem, Hawkstone, Prees, and Malpas, every evening by horse post, soon after the arrival of the London mail. THE STAMP OFFICE is kept in the Corn Market, as is also the SALOP FIRE OFFICE. The COLLECTOR'S OFFICE for the receipt of the excise duties, is held in Barker Street. The CLERK OF THE PEACE'S OFFICE is at the Town Hall.

Bankers.

Messrs. Beck, Dodson, Eatons and Beck, draw on Masterman and Co.

Messrs. Burton, Lloyd, Lloyd, and Salt, draw on Stephenson, Remmington, and Co.

Messrs. Rocke, Eyton, Campbell, and Bayley, draw on Robarts, Curtis, and Co.

The banks are open every day from ten o'clock till four.

Newspapers.

Two weekly Newspapers are published here.

Wednesday,—The Salopian Journal, at the Office in the Corn Market.

Friday,—The Shrewsbury Chronicle, at the Office on St. John's Hill.

Stage Coaches.

The number of coaches precludes our specifying each particularly, nor indeed would it be of much avail for any length of time, as they change so frequently. The following directions, however, give every necessary information to the stranger in the choice of his conveyance to any part of the kingdom.

From the LION COACH OFFICE.

Mail Coaches to London, Holyhead, Hereford, Chester, Newtown, and all the intermediate places. *Stage Coaches* to London, Holyhead, Manchester, Liverpool, Hereford, Bristol, Bath, Birmingham, Cheltenham, Aberystwith, and the towns and villages on the road, daily.

The TALBOT INN.

Stage Coaches run from this house to the places named before.

The BRITANNIA INN.

Stage Coaches to London, Birmingham, and Aberystwith.

Stage Waggons.

Waggons to London, Wolverhampton, Machynlleth, Dolgelley, and Montgomeryshire, from *Crowley and Co.* Mardol.

Waggons to Chester; Manchester, Ludlow, and Leominster, from *Maxon's Warehouse*, Mardol.

Waggons to Aberystwith, Llangollen, Bala, Wem Wharf, (from whence goods are conveyed by water to Liverpool, &c.) Holyhead, &c. from *Newton's General Waggon and Barge Warehouse*, Mardol Quay.

Water Conveyance.

Barges go frequently (two or three in a week) for Bridgnorth, Worcester, Gloucester, Chepstow, and Bristol, days uncertain, from the warehouses of Owners *Harwood, Bratton* and *J. Jones*, on Mardol Quay, also from the *Union Wharf*, St. Mary's Water Lane.

Hackney Chairmen.

Hackney Chairs, or as they are sometimes called *Sedans*, are to be had for conveyance within the town at a moderate rate.

Friendly and Benefit Societies

Of these there are a great number in Shrewsbury, which assemble agreeably to their rules at different public houses, and would be far too many for enumeration here. Suffice it to say that, the MASONIC SOCIETY, the most respectable of them, assembles monthly on Mondays, at the Crown Inn.

Inland Navigation.

The Severn has its source from a chalybeate spring on the eastern side of Plinlimmon, a mountain in Montgomeryshire, in North Wales, from whence rushing down with a swift current, and being joined by many smaller torrents, it presently appears considerable, and passing by Llanidloes and Newtown, becomes navigable at Pool Quay, where the Vyrniew joins it with a stream little inferior to its own; from thence proceeding gently forward to Shrewsbury, which it surrounds nearly in the form of an horseshoe, it flows on through a rich vale with many extensive windings, till it comes to Benthall Edge, by the way receiving into it the river Tern, which waters all the north of Shropshire. Here the Severn begins to be rapid, being pent up between two opposite hills, both very lofty and steep; and from thence to Bridgnorth and Bewdley, the channel is confined by high woody banks and rocky cliffs, which afford a variety of beautiful prospects. Afterwards it again glides pleasantly on through the fertile plains of Worcestershire, visiting in its way the city itself, and a little below is considerably augmented by the influx of the river Teme. This addition, however, is much inferior to that which it receives from its junction with the river Avon, at Tewkesbury. These two rivers thus united, pursue their course to Gloucester, and about fifty miles below that city are lost in the Bristol Channel.

This river, justly esteemed the second in Britain, is of great importance, being navigated by vessels of large burden, more than 160 miles from the sea, without the assistance of any lock. Upwards of 100,000 tons of coal are annually shipped from the collieries about Madeley and Broseley, for the cities and towns situate on its banks, and thence conveyed into the adjacent counties. Great quantities of grain, pig and bar iron, iron manufactures, Coalport china and earthenware, as well as wool, hops, cyder, and provisions, are likewise continually sent to Bristol and other places, from whence various kinds of goods are brought in return. In May, 1756, the number of Barges and Trows on the river Severn navigating from Shrewsbury downwards to Bristol amounted to 376, and since that time, by the addition of the inland canals from the Trent, the Mersey and the Thames, into the Stroud navigation, it may fairly be calculated that not less than double that number are now employed.

Shrewsbury Canal.

This canal commences on the north-east side of Shrewsbury, and winding with the Severn passes Uffington, where it runs parallel with the river Tern and passes Upton Forge, Withington, Roddington, where it crosses the river Roden, also the river Tern, at Long Mill; passes Long, Eyton, crosses Ketley Brook at Wrockwardine Wood, and there joins the Donnington Wood and the Shropshire Canals. The total length is 17½ miles; with 147 feet rise in the five miles between Long and Wombridge; the rest is level.—

The principal use of this canal is the conveyance of coals for the consumption of Shrewsbury and the intermediate places, from the numerous coal works in the eastern part of Shropshire, which furnish that article of an excellent quality. The best are delivered in Shrewsbury at about 15s. per ton.

ENVIRONS OF THE TOWN.

Sutton Spa.

QUITTING Shrewsbury by the suburb of Coleham, and proceeding for about a mile along a narrow lane, we reach Sutton Spa. Few countries in Europe can boast of more medicinal or mineral waters than England, the virtues of which have been well established, not from vulgar experience only, but from the repeated examinations of the most skilful physicians. The uncommon frequency of the healing springs may rationally be attributed to the lixivious quality of our rain water, to the variety of rich soils, with the spoils of which, from their property of dissolving, they must be fraught, and to the wonderful and inimitable chemistry of nature by which they are so happily impregnated as to become the easiest and surest remedies of the most grievous and otherwise incurable diseases.

For the following account of this Spa the author is indebted to a paper drawn up by Dr. Evans, (now of Llwynygroes,) and inserted in the Agricultural Survey of Shropshire by the Rev. Archdeacon Corbett:

> "Sutton Spa is situated about two miles south of Shrewsbury, on the slope of a gentle eminence, and close to a village of the same name. The spring issues from a rocky stratum of ash coloured clay, or argillaceous schistus, containing (as appears by its effervescence with nitrous acid) a small portion of lime. Fresh from the spring, the Sutton water is clear and colourless, and exales a slightly sulphureous smell; which is most perceptible in rainy weather. It sparkles little when poured into a glass, having no *uncombined* carbonic acid in its composition. When first drawn its strong salt taste is evidently mixed with a chalybeate flavour; but the latter is wholly lost on exposure for a few hours, bubbles of air separating slowly, and a reddish sediment lining the sides and bottom of the vessel.
>
> "The Sutton water has by many been compared with that of Cheltenham, and supposed to contain nearly the same ingredients. It bears, however, a much closer resemblance to sea-water, and has accordingly been found most beneficial in those cases for which sea-water is usually recommended.

"In the case of scrophula, the superior merits of sea-water has been uniformly and universally acknowledged. A similarity of ingredients would naturally lead us to expect similar effects from the Sutton water; and I am happy to bear testimony, that a twenty years practice at the Salop Infirmary, as well as in private practice, has furnished me with abundant proofs of its success in the treatment of scrophulous affections; and in addition to the properties possessed by the Sutton-spring in common with sea-water, it enjoys one evident advantage in containing iron. [108]

"The air of Sutton, as might be expected from its open elevated situation, is dry and wholesome. The site commands a rich and highly variegated prospect, bounded on one side by the magnificent group of Breyddin and Moel y Golfa, with a long range of Welsh mountains rising in full majesty behind them; and on the other by their no mean rivals, the Wrekin and Stretton Hills. The view of Shrewsbury, betwixt the branches of the adjoining wood, particularly when the setting sun gilds every object with his mellowest light, is greatly and most deservedly admired. The walk from Shrewsbury is pleasant and picturesque; and the neighbourhood of a reasonable and abundant market, can be considered as no trifling object, when compared with the extravagant prices and scanty accommodations of many of our remote watering-places."

Since the before-named estimable and respectable physician drew up the account (about 1801) of the Spa, from which the above is extracted, a neat cottage and baths for hot and cold bathing have been erected by the noble proprietor, provided with comfortable accommodations for invalids. We cannot help thinking, that "while almost every fishing village on the coast is preparing conveniences for sea-bathing, how desirable would it be to extend similar advantages to the interior parts of the island, where poverty or infirmity render it impossible to visit the distant sea."

The town is regained by a pleasant walk along the lane above the Spa, which leads the tourist into the Abbey Foregate, very near to the column erected in honour of Lord Hill.

Shelton Oak,

Stands about one mile and a half from Shrewsbury, just where the Pool road diverges from that which leads to Oswestry. This oak is remarkable, as well for its size as its traditional history. Owen Glyndwr is said to have ascended it at the battle of Shrewsbury to reconnoitre; but finding that the king had a numerous army, and that Northumberland had not joined his son Hotspur, he fell back to Oswestry, and, immediately after the battle, retreated precipitately into Wales.

The tree is now in a complete state of decay, even its larger ramifications; and within the hollow of it at bottom six persons at least may sit down and partake of refreshment.

Excursion to Haughmond Abbey and Uffington.

The pedestrian may, in this walk proceed either along the turnpike road or by the side of the river; we shall make choice, however, of the former, on account of its facility for the description of several interesting objects which present themselves on the route.

Proceeding from the town through the suburb of Castle Foregate, we leave the extensive linen factory of Messrs. Marshall, and Co. on the left, the monotonous noise from the machinery of which is very agreeably relieved by the pleasant and extensive view that presents itself, in conjunction with the bleaching fields belonging to Messrs. Benyons' factory on the right, and renders the prospect extremely interesting. At the distance of one mile from the town, on the left, is the Old Heath. Previous to the erection of the present excellent prison, all condemned malefactors expiated their offences by the sacrifice of their lives to the offended laws of their country in a field which adjoins the road at this place. Continuing our jaunt to the turnpike, and keeping to the right, at the distance of about 2½ mites from Shrewsbury we reach Sundorn Castle, the residence of Mrs. Corbet. The landscape in travelling along this road is exquisitely beautiful; rich corn fields and pastures demonstrate the fertility of the soil, watered by the majestic stream of the Severn, with a great number of rivulets which, descending from the uplands, pour their tributary streams into that river; while the pleasant seats and farm houses, thickly scattered through the scene in contemplation, and surrounded by clumps of trees and copse wood, satisfy the spectator that nature has not in this neighbourhood lavished her treasures in vain.

The elegant mansion of Sundorn was erected in the castellated style by the late John Corbet, Esq.: Its site in a beautiful lawn, the venerable appearance of the castle, the sloping banks which surround the large sheet of water covered with plantations, the rich verdure of the adjoining woods, numerous corn fields and pasture grounds tufted with trees, the hedgerows and walks happily arranged, the bold appearance of the castle on the adjoining hill, diversify the scene and render the *tout ensemble* extremely interesting.

Within the demesne of Sundorn, the remains of Haughmond Abbey are situated. Of the foundation of this once venerable pile there is now no entire trace. Of the Abbey-church, nothing remains but the south door of the nave, a most beautiful and highly adorned round arch, resting on slender shafts, between which on each side have been inserted a Gothic tabernacle, inclosing statues of St. Peter and St. Paul. The chapter-house is entire; it is oblong, with the upper end forming two sides of a hexagon. The roof is of fine oak, and above has been another story. The entrance is by a richly decorated round arch, with a window on each side, divided into two round arched compartments, by slender short pillars. The spaces between the shafts of these arches have Gothic niches, and statues of the Virgin Mary, Gabriel, St. Catherine, St. John, &c. South of the chapter house, and opposite the site of the church, are remains of the Refectory, and beyond a large building, consisting of a spacious hall, eighty-one feet by thirty-six, lighted by Gothic windows on each side, and a large one, once filled with tracery, at the west end. On the north side is a curious antique fire-place. Communicating with this, at the eastern extremity, and at right angles, is another apartment of nearly the same size, once evidently in two rooms. At the south end is an elegant bay window. It is conceived this building formed the abbot's lodgings and hall. The situation of the Abbey on a rising ground, backed by a noble distant forest, commands a very rich and extensive view of the great plain of Shrewsbury, with the town and castle, enriched by mountainous tracts.

Proceeding from the Abbey along the bottom of the wood, and ascending the hill, we reach a shooting box, erected in the form of an ancient turret, by the late Mr. Corbet. Near it Lord Douglas, in the battle of Shrewsbury, was taken prisoner, in attempting to precipitate himself down the steep, when his horse fell under him, and he received a severe contusion on the knee. On reaching the summit of this hill, the traveller will enjoy a beautiful prospect. His attention is lost in variety; and his imagination for a while suspends its powers in contemplating indiscriminately the vast but diversified assemblage. In this situation he will recollect with pleasure the animated lines of Thomson, whose descriptive genius must continue to do honour to his country, as long as taste and elegance are regarded.

> "Meantime you gain the height, from whose fair brow
> The bursting prospect spreads immense around,
> And snatch'd o'er hill, and dale, and wood, and lawn,
> And verdant fields, and darkening heath between,
> And villages embosom'd soft in trees,
> And spiring towns, by surging columns mark'd
> Of household smoke, your eye excursive roams,
> Wide stretching from the hall, [113] in whose kind haunt

> The hospitable genius lingers still,
> To where the broken landscape, by degrees
> Ascending, roughens into rigid hills."

The spectator, if he has any taste for the sublime and beautiful in nature, will find himself abundantly repaid for the labour of the ascent. His eyes will wander with pleasure over the beautiful villas, the retreat of the rich and affluent, diversified with woods and corn-fields, that present themselves on the fertile plain adjoining the hill. Immediately before him, he will discover the ancient town of Shrewsbury, with its lofty spires, its noble river and canal, whilst in the distance a range of green mountains, interspersed with woods, that seem to be carelessly scattered on their sloping sides, form a suitable background to this picturesque and interesting scene.

Descending from the hill, we immediately reach the pleasant village of Uffington, situated on the banks of the Severn, where at the Bowling Green excellent accommodations will be met with. From hence the canal and river side afford a pleasant walk, which reconducts us to our starting place—Shrewsbury.

Attingham Hall,

Distant about four miles on the London road, is built of beautiful free stone, and is situated in a very extensive lawn on the banks of the river Tern, over which is a handsome bridge erected by the late lord Berwick. The south front, which is upwards of 365 feet in length, has an extremely grand appearance; being decorated with lofty Ionic pilasters and a magnificent portico. The interior of the house has much to recommend it, particularly its lofty and spacious hall, the entablature of which is supported by Verd Antique Scaglioni columns, with statuary capitals and bases. The picture gallery is a spacious room 78 feet 6 inches long, by 25 feet 6 inches wide, and 24 feet high. It contains many *chef d'œuvres* of the old masters, particularly some valuable ones by Raffaello—Parmigiano—Paolo Veronese—Annibal Caracci—Rubens—Vandyck—Poussin—Kuyp—the Ostade's—Murillo—Salvator Rosa—Berchem. The walls of this elegant room are of a deep lake colour; the ceiling supported by porphyry columns of the Corinthian order, the capitals and bases of which are beautifully gilded. Underneath the cornice of this extensive room is a gold fringe of great depth. The floor is inlaid with rich Mosaic work, and the grand staircase is finished in a corresponding style of magnificence. The suite of drawing rooms is superbly furnished with immense plate glasses and burnished gold furniture, and the ceilings are richly gilt. The boudoir is a beautiful small circular room, the pannels of which are decorated by the pencil of one of our first artists. The library is in the west wing, and is a very extensive and lofty room, the cornice is supported by rich Corinthian pilasters; and besides a very valuable collection of books, it contains several rare specimens of sculpture from the antique. Among those most worthy notice is a font [115] from Hadrian's Villa; on the basso relievo on its exterior the story of Narcissus is beautifully told. A rich candelabra from the antique, of exquisite workmanship, near ten feet high—a fine colossal statue of Apollo Belvidere—a beautiful Esculapius—with a splendid collection of Etruscan vases from Herculaneum, busts, chimeras, &c. &c. The rooms on the first floor correspond in the grandeur and magnificence of their furniture with those on the ground floor.

The house was built originally from a design by Mr. Stewart, but it has lately undergone a very extensive alteration, under the superintendance of Mr. Nash; the rich and costly carvings and ornamental furniture, were executed by Mr. Donaldson, of Shrewsbury, whose correct taste in that fine art is too well appreciated to need any eulogium here.

The situation of the house is healthy and delightful; and the grounds contiguous thereto have lately been much improved. The view of this elegant seat, from the public road near the before-mentioned bridge has a fine effect: its beautiful front—the extensive shrubberies—with the park richly clothed with fine timber on the back ground, rising to a considerable height above the mansion; whilst in the distance on the left will be seen the pleasing village of Atcham—its parish church—and bridge, present, even to the passing stranger, a very pleasing scene. The gardens, walks and pleasure grounds, are laid out with taste, and display some very fine scenery.

Hawkstone,

The seat of the noble and celebrated family of the Hills, is situated on the eastern border of the county, about 14 miles from Salop, and though with regard to the surrounding country it may be said to stand on an extensive plain, it in itself consists of a group of prominent and astonishingly romantic rocks, forming by far one of the most attractive features, not only of this, but perhaps, taken altogether, of any other county. To attempt a particular or even a general description, would very far exceed the limits of our whole book, as a cursory inspection of its wonders occupies a walk of several days. General Paoli, who visited this place before the late improvements, publicly declared that in all his extensive travels, not even excepting Italy or Switzerland, there were some scenes here that surpassed in grandeur any thing he had seen.—A slight notice of some of its principal beauties will best become our humble efforts in so limited a work. The house, though spacious and elegant, and not of very ancient erection, notwithstanding it is embellished with some fine specimens of sculpture and painting, forms but a small part of what is sought after here; the attractive powers of Hawkstone consisting entirely in the enchantment of the surrounding scenery. Three or four massive rocks irregularly grouped, with their fine wooded sides disclosing at intervals abrupt crags, towers, and shelving precipices, with intermediate vallies of still seclusion and spreading lawns of verdant freshness, together with many a broad expanse of park, studded with luxuriant trees either grouped in groves, or single in feathery fullness, the whole enlivened by inhabitants appropriate, picture to the sight both at once and successively—scenes only equalled and seldom surpassed, even in the poetic regions of luxuriant romance.—The Grotto is approached through a stupendous natural chasm of great length, and narrowing till but one person at a time can pass, while over head the sky is just seen at a great height; a dark cavern is then passed, and the sky is again for a moment seen, when entering another cavern of complete darkness and gradual ascent, the grotto is, after considerable, though perfectly safe wandering, entered: the first appearance of this spacious cavern is truly sublime, as it is seen by the glimmering light of variously stained glass, throwing its lurid and sepulchral faintness on the massive pillars, till at length the grotto is entered with all its brilliance: It consists of a very extensive excavation, finely fretted to its termination with a profusion of rich petrifactions, shells, and marine productions. In one of its awful recesses, through an iron grate, is seen the figure of a British Druid, in complete costume, passing amid the massy pillars, in a dim and green light.—After various windings, a door suddenly opens in the summit of the precipice, where, over the shelving rocks below, and far above the highest forests, a scene of magnificence bursts on the eye exceeding almost conception. This height is with some difficulty descended by innumerable winding steps cut in the solid rock.

A SCENE in SWITZERLAND is presented here on the heathy summit of one of the mountains, where a narrow plank bridge crosses a deep chasm, and connects two rocks of terrific height and cragginess.

The terrace formed on the ridge of one of the hills, finely wooded, is terminated by an octagon summer-house, that commands a prospect of astonishing extent, from whence the bordering mountains of Wales, with parts of no less than 13 counties, are distinctly enumerated.—Near this place is a Column, 112 feet high, surmounted with a colossal statue of sir Rowland Hill, the first protestant lord mayor of London, in 1550, the 3rd year of Edward VI. In a most romantic glen, near this place, is an Urn, erected by the late sir Richard Hill, purporting that it was the hiding-place of one of his ancestors, during the civil wars of Edward I. while his house was ravaged by the parliament soldiers; but that his son speedily came to his assistance: the approach to and from it now is much facilitated, without destroying the wildness of the scene, by extensive passages and steps.

Beyond this is a well-stocked Menagerie of living Animals, principally birds.—From hence, round the sudden and abrupt corner of a rock, and through the cleft body of an old oak, is entered one of the sweetest vallies imagination can tint, and most properly called ELYSIUM: It is bounded completely by wooded and inaccessible rocks, and can only be entered at this narrow passage, or at the extreme termination of its extent, about half a mile.—On the most western of this group of rocks are the remains of RED CASTLE, built in the reign of Henry III., though it is mentioned by this name in a grant as ancient as William the Conqueror. It is now in awful ruins; but lofty fragments of its walls form some of the most picturesque beauties of this romantic place; and fling on the mind, if such scenes needed it, the additional charm of that strange feeling that antiquity and fallen grandeur never fail to excite. Amid these towers is a well of surprising depth; called now the GIANT'S WELL. The site of this castle is ascended and descended (as is usual amid most of the strange scenes here) by steps cut in the rocks; and very frequently through caverns, sometimes natural, but always surprising. At the bottom of one of these is suddenly seen a Lion in his den, which, though assuredly a trifling toy amid such scenery, never fails to astonish the generality of visitors.—Here is also a SCENE in OTAHEITE, consisting chiefly of a Hut, built exactly on the model of what our lamented countryman, Captain Cook witnessed in that happy island, and ornamented accordingly: the scene wherein it is erected first pointed out the propriety.

To enumerate, much more to describe, all, or even the principal attractions of this wonderful place, would, as we before stated, very far exceed the limits we have allotted thereunto: yet before we close, as we would willingly please readers of every description, it may not be amiss to notice what is not improperly called NEPTUNE'S WHIM, a spot no doubt most largely applauded by the generality of visitors here. It is very properly detached at a tolerable distance from the principal scenery of Hawkstone; and consists of a cottage ornamented with shell-work and cinders, amid ponds of fish; behind which is a mighty figure of the marine god, with a profuse current gushing through his urn; he is accompanied, of course, by his Tritons and Nereids, spouting water through their leaden shells. This is acknowledgedly *a whim* of his godship, whereof he partakes with mortals; nor can these trifles, or even some of the inscriptions, tend to lessen the august grandeur of this most magnificent spot, wherein art has had little more to do than clear a path, for the votaries of nature to have access to her most sportive and astonishing charms.

>   What skill, what force divine,
> Deep felt in these appear! a simple train,
> Yet so delightful mix'd, with such kind art,

Such beauty and beneficence combin'd;
Shade, unperceiv'd, so softening into shade;
And all so forming an harmonious whole;
That as they still succeed they ravish still.

THOMSON.

At the entrance to the Park is erected a very handsome and commodious Inn, capacious enough for the reception of a number of families; many of which frequently spend a considerable part of the summer in this delightful spot. The attention of the worthy host and the excellence of the accommodations, provisions and wines, must be experienced to be duly appreciated.

Howell, Printer.

FOOTNOTES.

[33] The Welsh word for the principality of Wales.

[89] A great quantity of human bones have from time to time been dug up in the grounds which surrounded this ancient friary, from which it appears probable that it was once used as a burying place for those who died of the plague, which frequently and severely visited this town. Phillips says that after the battle of Battlefield, between Henry IVth and Hotspur, "many persons of note were buried in the Black and Austin's Friars in Shrewsbury."

[108] Sutton-spring water:

	Grains.	
A wine gallon of Sutton-water contains of muriate of soda	1082	6
Ditto of lime, with an admixture of muriated soda	226	0
Carbonate of iron	0	5
Clay and silex	11	5
Total of solid contents	1320	0
	Cubic Inches.	
Carbonic acid	1.805	
Common air, contaminated with azote and sulphurated hydrogen gas	12.635	
Total of volatile contents	14.440	

[113] The hospitable and truly old English mansion of Mrs. Corbet, which is seen on the right hand.

[115] When the French took possession of Rome, this font was undergoing a repair at the statuary's, and was considered so valuable an antique, that the French Commissary priced it at 2000 guineas. Being claimed however by the statuary as his own property, he was allowed to retain it, and afterwards he contrived to convey it to Lord B. to whom it belonged.

Milton Keynes UK
Ingram Content Group UK Ltd.
UKHW030956261124
451585UK00005B/723